Me and Jezebel

**WHEN
BETTE DAVIS
CAME FOR
DINNER—AND
STAYED...
AND STAYED...
AND STAYED...
AND...**

ELIZABETH FULLER

BERKLEY BOOKS, NEW YORK

ME AND JEZEBEL: WHEN BETTE DAVIS CAME FOR
DINNER AND STAYED . . .

A Berkley Book / published by arrangement with
the author

PRINTING HISTORY
Berkley edition / May 1992

ISBN: 0-425-13264-1

A BERKLEY BOOK ® TM 757,375
Berkley Books are published by The Berkley Publishing Group,
200 Madison Avenue, New York, New York 10016.
The name "BERKLEY" and the "B" logo
are trademarks belonging to Berkley Publishing Corporation.

PRINTED IN THE UNITED STATES OF AMERICA

10 9 8 7 6 5 4 3 2 1

To my spiritual guides,
Anita and Frank Hall.

AUTHOR'S NOTE

All the events on the following pages took place exactly as written, at my home in Weston, Connecticut, between May 28 and July 2, 1985.

Every incident and character is real, without distortion.

Me and Jezebel

1

THE STAR

I was standing in the front doorway, leaning against the sill, when I saw the stretch limo pull into our gravel driveway. The sleek supercar seemed to be a hundred feet long in front of our modest Connecticut cottage. Inside the limo, barely visible through the one-way window, Bette Davis was sitting in regal elegance. I saw my husband approach the car with the timid deference of a footman. I gave myself a reality check. Yes, it *was* Bette Davis. She *was* in our driveway. She *was* going to be our houseguest.

As the chauffeur opened the door, her face peeked out at me with the arrogance of Jezebel, the haughtiness of Margo Channing, and the petulance of Baby Jane. I was frantically trying to decide whether I should be friendly or obsequious in greeting the woman whom I had idolized for more than half my life, whom I had smothered with fan letters dripping with adoration. I was amused at the old letter I had found:

Dear Miss Davis, [*I had written at the age of thirteen*]

Thank you for the postcard with your picture on it. Now I have six of them. I have them lined up on my dresser. I had seven, but I gave one to my grandmother for her birthday. She is a big fan of yours too.

Last week I was going through my grandmother's old collection of *Modern Screen* and it said that you had turned down the part of Scarlett O'Hara in *Gone With the Wind*. Is that true? I think Vivien Leigh did a good job, but you would have been much more superior.

My grandmother promised to take me to see *Jezebel* again the next time our movie house runs "Bette Davis Week." I'm sure that one wasn't approved in the *Catholic Universe Bulletin*, but my grandmother doesn't go by that paper—she thinks it's a bunch of hogwash.

My grandmother said that if God didn't want us to see Bette Davis movies, he wouldn't have given *you* talent and given *her* the extra fifty cents for us to go to the movies. You'd like my grandmother. She's her own person just like you. It doesn't matter to her who's Catholic and who isn't.

Oh yes, my grandmother and I were in the beauty parlor the other day and we read in *Silver Screen* that your fourth marriage is on the rocks. We will be lighting candles to Saint Anne, patron of all difficulties.

One last favor, I was wondering if you could send me and my grandmother a picture of you as Empress Catherine in your new movie?

Yours truly,
Elizabeth Brancae, 7th grader at
St. Louis Academy
Cleveland Heights, Ohio

Now, twenty-five years later, the circumstances leading to Bette Davis's unlikely stay at our house began when I had invited my friend Robin Brown for dinner. Although Robin is a contemporary of Bette's, we are close friends. Robin and Bette are the best of friends, too. They have been "chums," as they called themselves, since they first met as teenagers in Ogunquit, Maine. There Robin was working for the summer as a waitress at the Sparhawk Hotel to help pay college expenses. Bette was on vacation with her photographer mother, Ruthie.

The following summer the two teenagers, along with Ruthie and Bette's sister, Barbara, shared a summer cottage in the center of Ogunquit, a popular resort. In the mornings and early afternoons, Robin and Bette would sunbathe, wade ankle-deep in the frigid Maine waters, and fantasize about the day when they would become actresses on the Broadway stage. In the afternoons they were waitresses at Mrs. Johnson's Tea Room. "Bette and I had a 'snap' job," Robin recalled. "For a few hours each day we served cinnamon toast and tea to old ladies wrapped in shawls on the veranda. I'll never forget one day when Bette was serving tea to an elderly lady and got the giggles. They were infectious."

Robin went on to add, "I heard those *same* giggles years later when Bette played Mildred, the tawdry waitress in *Of Human Bondage*. No doubt Bette drew on her experience at Mrs. Johnson's Tea Room for that part."

That was about as much as Robin ever told me about Bette. Robin was very tight-lipped when it came to sharing the juicy stuff. It was probably the main reason why their friendship endured for more than half a century and why, whenever Bette was in the East, she would stay at Robin's house, a typical New England clapboard that smacked of Yankee traditions to the bone.

The day I phoned to invite Robin for dinner she dropped her voice and said, "Bette's staying with me. Can I ask her to tag along?"

What a question! Bette Davis *tagging* along? I was in pure ecstasy. The first lady of the silver screen was going to be in my house, eating my food, God forbid! Suddenly I was a frazzled wreck. I tortured myself with thoughts that my house was not big enough, clean, or posh enough. I reminded myself of what my mother said the first time she stepped inside our front door: "Has your decor been inspired by reruns of 'Little House on the Prairie'?" But these problems were dwarfed by an even bigger one: what on earth would I *say* to Bette Davis?

For longer than I can remember I had fantasized meeting The Legend. As a teenager growing up in the suburbs of Cleveland I had built an endless chain of fantasies, everything from being on Hollywood's back lot with the erratic and tempestuous star, to having lunch with her in the commissary, where she would viciously suck in a chestful of Lucky Strike smoke as she berated her current producer, director, and fellow actors. But for me she would be sweet and benevolent. Admittedly it was a stretch, but I created the fantasy in full, living color anyway.

Halfway into the dinner, I got up the courage to speak. With a marked tremolo in my voice, I asked, "Miss Davis, I read somewhere that one of your favorite lines is from *All About Eve* when Margo turns to her guests and says: 'Fasten your seat belts—it's going to be a bumpy flight!' "

Before I even had a chance to regret opening my mouth, she attacked with all the venom and fire of Margo Channing herself.

"*Keee-ryst*! You and everyone else have that line wrong!" she spouted in her staccato speech. Her eyes were popped like Ping-Pong balls. I quickly got the picture of what the song, "She's Got Bette Davis Eyes," meant.

"Margo said, 'Fasten your seat belts—it's going to be a bumpy *night*!' "

Once the record was set straight, she smashed her cigarette into the ashtray to punctuate her annoyance. I felt as if my heart were extinguished along with it. Only minutes later, however, she turned to me and said in her too precise diction: "Something certainly smells delicious." Then she smashed another half-smoked cigarette into the ashtray. I realized that I might be reading too much into that mannerism.

The dinner continued with a mood of edginess that ebbed and flowed with Bette's steady stream of brittle commentary, regardless of the subject matter. Both my husband, John, and I were guilty of attempting to create conversation on subjects we knew little or nothing about. This did not go unnoticed.

"*Gawd!*" she said, moving her hand like a window washer, "your abysmal lack of knowledge about Warner Brothers, William Wyler, and George Brent is enough to make me want to *vaaahmit!*"

I looked across the table at John. He gulped and then in an attempt to recuperate our status said, "That must have been an interesting old house of yours in New Hampshire?"

John was referring to a barn she had converted years earlier.

"Butternut was a *lovely* place," Bette said almost congenially. "But it framed some of the more *ghastly* episodes in my life!"

John was not about to give up yet. As a journalist he was just plain stubborn and at times just plain stupid. The next thing that flowed from his lips stunned even me.

"By the way, Bette," he said, helping himself to a chicken leg, "whatever happened to Gary Merrill?"

Gary Merrill was Bette's fourth, former, and last husband.

In a fraction of a second, she dropped a heavy ladle filled with gravy down on her dish. Deadly silence descended over the table.

By the time we finished the main course, I was convinced that she was having about as good a time as Joan Crawford had when Bette served up the roasted rat on a silver platter.

Shortly after the blueberry pie and coffee were served, Bette announced in a stentorian tone, "I have the utmost *disdain* for guests who don't know when it's time to go home."

With that, she swept up her silver cigarette case and her Bic lighter and added, "And *brother*, have I seen a lot of those types of human clay."

That night I drifted off to sleep in a roseate haze, content with bathing in reflected glory. John, however, went to bed chewing Maalox tablets.

The following day the phone rang. John answered it. It was unmistakably Bette Davis.

"Darling," she said to John over the phone, "I've *never* in my life asked anyone this before. But I'm in a real bind. There's a hotel strike going on in the city. Robin suddenly has to leave for Maine. I was wondering if it would put you and Elizabeth out too much if I spent a night or possibly two?"

I was in the backyard cooling my feet in our four-year-old son Christopher's wading pool when John came out and announced that Bette Davis would be arriving the following afternoon.

After my shock wore off, John asked if she had given any indication at all the night before that she might want to stay. I reminded him that, if anything, it appeared to be the other way around. Her exit line was: "Thank you for a pleasant dinner." Then she tapped her black cane on the floor and added, "The chicken was so raw it nearly pecked me."

I was convinced that we had not only ticked her off, but might have even poisoned her. John appeared as puzzled as I on why she chose our house, a cross between an English pub, a Vermont barn, and a chicken shed. The reality was, our house did not have any of the accoutrements Bette Davis was accustomed to. Of that I was sure.

Our guest sofa bed had been bought at a garage sale. It pulled out at a ten-degree angle. The deck that ran around the entire back of the cottage was held up by pure luck and a half dozen rotted posts. John had plunged through a powdery plank up to his kneecap the week before. My father, an insurance man, once commented that anyone visiting our house should consider taking out an extended life insurance policy with a double-indemnity clause to cover accidental death.

But what haunted me the most was that in less than twenty-four hours, the serene cottage that Bette was picturing would soon be overrun with lumber trucks, carpenters, and the buzzing of electric saws from eight in the morning to five in the afternoon.

I called our builder and pleaded with him to postpone the project. In his direct Yankee way he said, "If I postpone your project, I'll throw off my schedule to the middle of next year." Then he added, "You'd better keep a close eye on your 'special guest' if she goes out on that thing you call a deck. That's nothing more than a banquet table for termites!"

As our builder spoke, my mind flashed to what Bette had said the night before: "What a pleasure it must be to sit on this deck with the sound of the rushing river."

Then there was the ever-present problem of how to keep our four-year-old from acting his age. The night Bette came to dinner, I had carefully planned his schedule so that he would be sound asleep by the time she and Robin arrived. This was no easy feat. At six-thirty, when Christopher was at the peak of a sugar high, John took him outside and ran him up and down the backyard until John's bad knee locked up. I certainly couldn't expect him to do that routine again.

John and I ate dinner in reflective silence. I could tell John was ambivalent about our larger-than-life guest. Earlier in the day he had come in from mowing the lawn, flopped onto the sofa, and said, "If one dinner could heavily resemble the Battle of the Bulge, I can only imagine what a full twenty-four hours is going to be like."

I told John that I felt certain that once she was actually our houseguest, she would soften. Then the real Bette Davis would shine forth.

"Liz, are you saying that that impatient, explosive, extravagant, self-centered, and forceful woman who ate 'undercooked' chicken here last night was really Mother Teresa in disguise?"

"I simply said that if you take the time to read between the lines the way I do then you'll see a kindhearted, benevolent woman who just wants to be loved as much as everyone else."

"She's a model of human selflessness," John said, dropping his glasses to the tip of his nose. "Liz, my love, *you* are star struck!"

"Maybe so," I admitted, "but I also know that famous people feel as if they have to keep up the act until they get to feel comfortable with their surroundings."

"And where does all your pop psychology come

from?" John asked. "Have you been watching too many episodes of 'Lifestyles of the Rich and Famous'?"

"Very funny," I said, "It's all so obvious. Bette Davis was simply giving us our money's worth. If she had come in as 'herself' we would have been terribly disappointed."

"*You* would have been disappointed," John said. "I wouldn't have wakened at two in the morning fishing for the antacid."

"We just have to be a little more cautious about the topics of conversation," I warned.

"It'll be like living with the CIA," John said.

"By the way," I said, "Robin mentioned that whatever we do, *don't* discuss the obvious. Like 'Gee Bette, it looks like rain today' or 'What a lovely sunny day.' She *abhors* small talk."

"Did Robin give you any more helpful hints on how we should behave in our own home?"

"As a matter of fact she did. It's best if we don't ask her about her health, former marriages, her movies that bombed, coactors—especially Joan Crawford—and most of all, don't mention *anything* about the scandalous book her daughter just wrote about her."

"I can see that the next two days will be chock-full of folksy memories," John grumbled as he headed upstairs to his office, where he was desperately trying to meet a deadline on his new book about a killer tornado.

"Just think of how lucky we are," I called to John. "How many people can say that their idol actually stayed in their very own home?"

"She's your idol, Liz!"

• • •

The following morning the chauffeured limousine pulled up in front of our cottage. Before Bette had a chance to step out, the Fairfield Lumber truck slammed on its hissing airbrakes behind the limo.

"You wanna get that thing outta here?" a husky sort of voice called out from the cab of the truck. "Or do you want me to just dump this timber in the middle of the road?"

John was standing at the limousine ready to offer Bette his hand as she stepped out from the backseat. "The limo will be gone in a minute," John called to the truck driver with a slightly strained voice.

"What an enchanting cottage!" Bette said as she lifted her black pumps over the gravel, refusing John's help. "I'm not a cripple, for godsake!"

As the First Lady of the Silver Screen approached, the words of the song Shirley MacLaine made popular raced through my head: "If they could see me now . . . that old gang of mine . . ."

The song triggered a flashback to 1964. I was a senior at Cleveland Heights High School, in drama class, performing a skit as Bette Davis in *Whatever Happened to Baby Jane*. My grotesque overacting had brought the house down. Now, I suddenly wondered what *had* happened to my old gang. If only they could have seen me now, about to play hostess to Bette Davis. Bette and I would soon be chatting about Hollywood, directors, scripts, and about what to have for lunch.

"Now I don't want anyone to fuss," Bette said the moment she came through the front door. She ignored the sound of lumber being dumped twenty feet behind her. But she did not ignore a rather shaky front stoop.

"That front stoop needs attention," she said with a faint suggestion of Jezebel in her tone.

"Miss Davis," I said, reaching out a rather shaky hand toward her. "John and I are so happy you're going to stay with us."

The Grande Dame allowed me to pull the tips of her fingers toward me. Her reluctantly extended hand felt like a terminally ill trout.

There was no doubt about it: her commanding aura more than made up for her lost youthfulness. Her lips were well endowed with her trademark— ruby red lipstick generously smeared beyond the natural lip line. Her hyperthyroid blue eyes were still hypnotic. In fact they seemed to shout, "More than fifty years of success and still counting!"

She moved through our narrow entranceway, all the while commenting on how charming our house was in the daytime. Drugged with her presence, I blurted, "We thought that when you saw the house in the daylight you might say: 'What-A-*Dumpp*!' "

"For *chrissake*," she said, puckering up the ruby-reds. "I'm *exhausss-ted* with people who misconstrue that line. I didn't exclaim, 'What-A-*Dumpp*!' I simply muttered in an undertone to myself, 'What a dump.' It was a throwaway line!"

After that was settled, we showed Bette to our guest room. It was simple but ample with weathered pine paneling, old beams, and a cozy fireplace.

"I'm afraid our old pullout sofa has a rather rakish angle to it," John said. He took a long, thoughtful drag on his pipe at the exact time Bette took a short, unthoughtful drag on her cigarette.

"Now darlings, you're not to worry about me," she said with a pleasantness that until then had evaded me. "I'm only going to be here a couple or three days."

A couple or three days! That was a jolt. What happened to the *one* or maybe *two* days she told John over the phone?

John glared at me as if I were responsible for adding the extra day.

As I was mulling that one over, Bette picked her way across the cluttered room to the sliding glass door that leads to the deck. With her cigarette rotating like a propeller on an old Piper Cub, she peered out toward the river.

"Darlings," she said, "I think it will be just delightful to have lunch out here on the deck. At that charming table with the Cinzano umbrella. Don't you agree?"

"Gee Bette, I'm afraid that deck's a little bit shaky," John said, restoking his pipe.

"Brother, your front stoop isn't due for a good housekeeping award either," she grumbled.

"I've got an idea," I said, spineless. "Why don't we have lunch down by the river?"

"In black fly season?" John asked.

"*Gawd*, how I detest insects!" she said. "Nature's curse!"

Our lunch plans were suddenly interrupted by the livery man, who called from the doorway.

"Excuse me," he said in a subservient voice, "where would Miss Davis like her bags placed? The station wagon carrying them has just arrived."

Once again John glared at me, as if I was also supposed to know why a separate vehicle had arrived exclusively carrying her luggage.

"I'll come out and help," John said, leaving me alone with my temperamental idol.

"Miss Davis," I said timorously, "I cleared out the downstairs closet for your belongings."

"Very thoughtful," she said in her clipped signature voice.

I hadn't yet peeked out the window to see the packed station wagon bulging with what looked like the entire inventory of Mark Cross. Our guest closet would barely hold a simple garment bag.

Earlier in the day I had made a mental list of acceptable conversation. Food, I felt, could be safe conversational territory.

"I made New England clam chowder," I told Bette. "We'll have it with a salad and French bread."

"I *adorrre* clam chowder," Bette said, flinging a lighted cigarette into the fireplace.

"You like clam chowder?" I asked. I was unable to mask my delight. I had actually chosen just the perfect lunch.

Bette's response was to widen her eyes and stare at me as if to say, "That's just what I said, wasn't it!"

While John and the chauffeur were filing in with the luggage, I excused myself and went to the kitchen to begin preparing lunch. Just as I slid the loaf of French bread under the broiler, Bette appeared. She slammed a book down on the butcher block counter so hard that I jumped. I looked up to see that it was her daughter's newly published book, *My Mother's Keeper*.

"I would like you to read this," she said. "My daughter, B. D., sent it to me. *Just* what a mother needs after three goddam strokes, a mastectomy, and a broken hip!"

I was speechless. I didn't know how to react. I certainly had never expected her to bring up anything so personal.

"Wait till you read my lovely daughter's inscription," Bette said. Her eyes were bulging to create that Bette Davis look. "She says she's praying for me to accept the Lord into my life. As if I don't have enough problems in my life . . ."

I made no comment.

"My little girl has found religion," Bette said in a fiery tone. "B. D. thinks I'm a heathen. A sinner, for chrissake!"

I panicked. I didn't know how to tell Bette that by pure coincidence I was in the throes of writing an objective journalistic book about a gospel singer and healer. In less than one hour she was due to arrive at my house for one of our regular interview sessions.

Throughout lunch Bette carried on a running monologue. She dwelled completely on the destructiveness of religious fanaticism.

"Nothing is more re-vollll-ting than those TV evangelists who are making a goddam *killing* in the name of religion. Hypocrites! Ten years ago I played the mother of Aimée Semple McPherson. One minute she was preaching and the next she was whoring around. She was nothing but a *whore*! She made Joan Crawford look like Mary Poppins . . ."

The moment we finished lunch, I phoned the healer about whom I was writing on assignment from my publisher. The healer was known only by the name of Grace. I explained to Grace the sensitive situation with Bette, her daughter, and the religion thing. I told Grace that although we were on a tight deadline, I felt that under the circumstances it would be a good idea if we simply postponed our interview sessions until Bette left—in two or three days.

This did not go over well with Grace. She had her heart set on meeting Bette Davis. I was caught in an unsought balancing act. There was simply no tactful way to keep the two from meeting. I did, however, beg Grace to lay low on the Jesus paraphernalia.

By midday Bette was unpacked. She stood at the living room window, twirling a freshly lit cigarette and admiring the alleged tranquillity of our New England cottage.

"This is such a welll-come relief from that stifling suite at the Ritz," she said. Then she added, "If I had to suffer one more bloody fire truck or siren, I would have gone *maaahd*!"

Bette did not yet know anything about Grace, nor had I broken the news that the carpenters were due to arrive at eight o'clock the next morning for weeks of renovation.

I was in the kitchen defrosting a chicken when I heard Bette gasp, "What the *hell* is in your drive-way?"

Grace had pulled up in her van. The front bumper sticker read: Honk for Jesus.

Grace was striking. She looked like a dark-haired

Loni Anderson. In addition, she had a voice that had won her a full scholarship to the Juilliard School of Music. While Grace walked up the driveway, I quickly began to explain her to Bette.

"Grace is really a dedicated lady," I began. "She's nothing like Aimée Semple McPherson or any of those other phonies. I've got a contract to write her life's story. Grace's healings are documented by top medical doctors . . ."

Bette's eyes almost left their orbits as I talked.

The first thing Grace said after entering was, "Miss Davis, I have a few things I'd like to give you."

Bette stiffened and stared in an icy silence that would have given Baby Jane the chills.

Grace spoke with all the eagerness of an evangelist on the brink of a conversion: "I have a Bible, a Jesus pinky ring, and a book called *God Wants You to Be Happy*."

"Young lady," Bette said, maintaining frightening eye contact, "your Bible, book, and Jesus pinky ring will have to find a new home!"

With those words, Bette smashed her cigarette into the corner of the cheese dish, ashes flying everywhere. Then she folded her arms and glared at both of us.

"Who would like coffee?" I asked, quivering.

"Give me a vodka and orange juice!" Bette commanded. "And after that, Elizabeth, you and I will go out for a drive."

My interview with Grace came to an abrupt end. Grace got back into her van. Bette got into our old two-door Toyota. We drove along the winding Connecticut roads framed with the traditional tumbledown dry walls. Her silence made me wish for a few sardonic remarks. But they did not come. Finally I spoke.

"Is there any place you would particularly like to go?"

"*Anywhere* as long as we don't meet up with your friend the evangelist. *Christ*, I thought she was never going to leave. Deliver me from Jesus pinky rings . . ."

"I'll make certain that Grace doesn't come back while you're still here," I said, speaking like the equerry to Her Majesty the Queen.

"That's thoughtful," she said, dismissing our current conversation.

I suddenly looked at my watch and realized that it was time to pick up Christopher from preschool. I asked Bette if she would mind this little detour. She answered with noncommittal silence.

Christopher squirmed into his car seat. "This is Miss Bette Davis," I told him formally. "Can you say hello?"

He clamped his lips together and then said bluntly, "No!"

Bette, however, in an unexpected jab of cordiality, said, "It's a pleasure to meet you, young man."

Christopher responded by thumping the back of Bette's front seat with the toes of his Captain Power sneakers. Then he ordered in his four-star general's voice: "Take me to McDonald's!"

"Christopher, if you don't stop kicking the back of Miss Davis's seat you'll never go to McDonald's for a dinosaur's age."

"You promised!" he screeched and kicked the seat again.

Bette winced. "For chrissake take him to McDonald's!" She snapped the ashtray closed.

"Tell her smoking is bad for her," Christopher said.

"Jeeezus!" Bette muttered under her breath.

"Miss Davis, I'm really sorry for all this," I apologized, "but I did promise him." I ground my molars together and drove on, cringing at the image of Bette Davis walking on McDonald's eternally wet tile floors while strident voices shouted food orders over loudspeakers, and toddlers weaved in and out of the food lines.

We arrived at the golden arches in a few minutes. I helped Bette out of the car while Christopher spun between us and succeeded in knocking Bette's cane out of her hand. I reached down, picked it up, and caught the swinging door just in time to stop it from knocking Bette back into the parking lot.

I found an empty booth next to the kiddy rides, snatched some crumbled napkins and swirled them fruitlessly over the puddles of used catsup on the table. Then I told Bette to have a seat and I would be right back with Christopher's kiddy pack. I couldn't imagine Bette Davis sinking her teeth into a Big Mac, but I asked her if she might like a snack of some sort.

The rolling of her poached-egg eyes heavenward said *No!* I plucked Christopher off the merry-go-round and carried him on my hip to the counter.

Once back at the table, I dumped the squirming Christopher in the booth, opposite Bette. He ripped the kiddy pack open, looking for its toy surprise. It was a plastic car. He wanted an airplane. A full-blown tantrum followed.

Christopher could sense my anxiety. He performed the dreaded holding-of-the-breath act that never failed to alarm me and everyone in his path.

"For chrissakes, *do* something!" Bette blasted, capturing the attention of half of McDonald's. "He's turning *blue*!"

For a split second, I felt as if that might be one solution. I took his puffy little tear-soaked face between my hands and said, "Mister, this is unacceptable behavior."

Suddenly I noticed Bette staring at something behind me. I turned quickly and saw a cluster of women. They were fixated on Bette Davis, deadly shocked that she would be in a booth at McDonald's wreathed in cigarette smoke and nibbling on a tiny piece of Christopher's Ronald McDonald cookie.

Then I looked behind Bette. Several more fans were approaching, hell-bent on seeing their movie star in the flesh. Both sides had now drawn pencils and paper and were closing in for her autograph.

"Oh, Miss Davis," one woman of about forty said, "*Dark Victory* is my all-time favorite movie."

"*Of Human Bondage* is mine," giggled her friend, who had a fourteen-year-old daughter with her.

"Who's that lady?" the daughter whispered to her gaping mother.

"So you don't know who I am, young lady!" Bette said, shifting into an even higher gear. "My grandson was *thrilll-ed* when the song 'She's Got

Bette Davis Eyes' came out. Then he was *sure* that his grandmother had indeed made it!"

"I've got that record," the girl said. "But Kim Carnes sang it. And you're not Kim Carnes!"

"*I am Bette Davis!*" Bette Davis said without a trace of false modesty.

"Wow!" the girl said. "Can I have your autograph too?"

While Bette perfunctorily signed autographs to the whispering and giggling cluster, an elderly couple having coffee at the next booth called over. "Excuse us," the husband said. "Mind if I ask you just one question, Miss Davis?"

"Shoot," Bette said in between ferocious puffs on her ever-present stage device.

The man gave a nervous chuckle and asked, "Harriet here wants to know if you ever said, 'Petah, Petah, Petah'?"

"*Nooooo!*" Bette groaned. "And Grant *never* said, 'Juday, Juday, Juday,' and Bogart *never* said, 'Play it again, Sam.' "

Revealing that bit of firsthand Hollywood trivia, Bette crushed out her cigarette, gathered her cane and black alligator handbag, and then held out her hand for me to help her slide out of the booth.

With both Christopher and Bette in tow, I plunged toward the exit and whisked them across the parking lot to my car.

"I'm so sorry," I said as I started the car. "I never expected you to be bothered like that."

"I never expected it *not* to happen," Bette said. "I'm sick to my stomach of all those celebrities who pretend to not enjoy being recognized. When they stop wanting your autograph, you're *finished*. *Finished*!"

"So you really didn't mind all that?" I asked, suddenly aware that that was what she had just told me.

Fortunately she wasn't on the attack. In fact for the first time since she arrived—five hours earlier—she was actually bordering on friendliness. I wondered if her mood swing was due to some sort of adrenaline high, induced by fan worship. I knew *my* adrenaline was pumping.

"*Christ*!" Bette blasted, "at that gala of stars in New York last year, Paul Newman *refused* to give one autograph. 'No,' Mr. Newman said, 'I don't give autographs.' Big fucking deal!"

"Mommy, Miss Davis just said the F word," Christopher called from his car seat, where he was happily playing with the toy car.

"Christopher," I said, "tend to your own business."

"Christopher is absolutely right," Bette said, sharply drawing in a lungful of smoke. "I shall not use any more 'F' words in front of little ears."

Moments later she said: "Shit, every time I think of how Newman *refused* to sign autographs, I want to vaahmit! At the end of the evening Newman said, 'Bette, we were once neighbors in Connecticut. We should get together for dinner one evening.' And I said, 'What for!' " Bette broke into a hearty but clipped laugh.

As I drove home my mind raced between exaltation and desperation. I was exalted that Bette Davis was riding shotgun with me in the car, sharing an inside look at Paul Newman, but I was desperate that a repeat performance of that fiasco in Mc-Donald's would spring up again.

Storm clouds were brewing on the horizon. Human storm clouds. Our builder, Grover Mills, and his carpenter, Skipper, were due to arrive first thing in the morning, before our houseguest had a chance to open those Bette Davis eyes. Grover and Skipper approached every job with the enthusiasm of Batman and Robin taking over Gotham City.

I could only cringe at the thought of what would happen the next morning when they began their anvil chorus within a few feet of where Bette was sleeping.

2

HELL'S HOUSE

Predictably, Grover and Skipper began work exactly on schedule. At eight o'clock sharp, they chose a place some six feet away from Bette's room. Two saw-screeches and five hammer blows later, Bette slipped out of her room and into the kitchen. She was wearing a short, silky nightie. She appeared oblivious of the fact that John was sitting at the table finishing his breakfast. He looked like a startled fawn caught in the headlights of an oncoming car.

"It was so kind of you and John to take me in," Bette said with brittle cheer. She made no comment about the noise of the back deck being ripped down just ten feet away.

"Liz darling, would you mind *terribly* picking up some Carnation Instant Breakfast drink, chocolate flavored, a carton of Vantage cigarettes, and the

Daily News?" Bette asked, widening her unmade-up blue eyes.

The only thought going through my head was that Bette Davis had been in my house less than twenty-four hours and not only was she calling me "Liz" but "Liz darling." Euphoric, I transported myself back to when I was twelve years old, when my grandmother and I walked to Walgreens for a cherry Coke and a pretzel stick. Suddenly she jerked her size four box-toed pumps to an abrupt halt in front of the Cleveland Heights movie theater, and announced with unrestrained enthusiasm, "Now *there's* talent!"

In front of us was a life-size poster of Bette Davis promoting *Jezebel* as the main attraction for Bette Davis Week. The black-and-white poster depicted her in a satin gown trimmed in lace and velvet that I immediately lusted after.

"I bet that dress cost fifty dollars," I said to my grandmother, who was straining to see the fine detail around the neck.

"Honey," my grandmother said, taking my small hand in her even smaller, wrinkled hand, "for your sweet sixteen birthday, I'm going to buy you a dress just like that one."

"Where are you going to get the money for that, Grandma?"

"Never you mind about that!" she said, half scolding me for doubting that she would come through with the dress.

I was brought back to the present when Grover Mills appeared at the kitchen bar. Seeing him standing there, complete with baseball cap and tool belt, Bette stepped back with distinct surprise. She swirled toward me for an explanation of why a builder came in without knocking.

Bette was not yet familiar with Grover and the way he would take over our house during each renovation project. "All we need is for Aimée Semple McPherson to return so we can have a party!" Bette barked. Then she struck a match on the underside of our kitchen table.

Grover was not at all fazed by the Living Legend standing in her flimsy nightie on the other side of the bar. He was, however, startled when she struck a kitchen match on the underside of his newly built oak table. He dropped on one knee to search for a possible scorch mark. Finding one, he groaned, gave it a cursory once-over with sandpaper, and then went to the refrigerator, where he helped himself to a prune Danish to go with his coffee. After scrounging around in the refrigerator, he commented, "We're out of cream and mayo, you know?"

Bette didn't speak. But the pop of her eyes indicated that she would not suffer Grover and his familiarity for long.

"Well, I guess I'll run to the store," I said, not wanting to get involved with the standoff between Bette and Grover.

As I headed out to the car, John followed. He spoke softly through the open driver's window. "Did Bette give you any money?"

"No," I said casually.

"There's more than ten dollars involved here," he whispered.

"So?" I said, annoyed at John because he was bothered about a trivial ten-dollar purchase when the most important star in the universe was concerned.

"Liz, it's *not* the money. It's the principle of the thing. She should have at least offered."

"You're being ridiculous."

"You're blind," John said. "In my book, you don't send your hostess off shopping without paying for your stuff."

"I'm sure she'll pay me when I get back," I said, cutting him off.

"I wish I shared your confidence," John said.

"I wish you shared my diplomacy."

"What do you mean by that?" John asked, feigning naivete.

"Don't play dumb."

"Are you referring to last night?" John asked. "The dinner from hell?"

"You got it," I said. "I couldn't believe my ears when you turned to Bette like a psychotherapist and said, 'Tell me, Bette, did you and Joan Crawford ever resolve your conflict before she died?' "

"I was curious to know," John said. "I'm an investigative journalist."

"With all the subtlety of Geraldo Rivera."

"I only asked her because if she didn't bury the hatchet, it could eat away at her," John said.

"But that's none of our concern! Robin specifically told us that we weren't to ask her about Joan Crawford," I said.

"I don't care if it's Bette Davis or Betty Crocker. I'm not going to be censored in my own home!"

"So you didn't ask her out of genuine concern," I said. "You were trying to stir up trouble."

"Stirring up trouble with Bette Davis is to ask her: 'How are you today?' She never acted a role in her life."

"Do me a favor," I said. "Let's just try to make the next forty-eight hours as pleasant as possible."

"It's a two-way street," John mumbled as he walked toward the house.

When I returned home from the store, I was relieved to find John in his office, safely tucked away from Bette at the opposite end of the house. I gingerly tapped on the door to Bette's room.

"It's only me, Miss Davis," I called. "I've got your cigarettes, Carnation Breakfast drink, and the *Daily News.*"

She whisked the door open. "Thank *Gawd* you're back!" she said, exhaling a cloud of smoke.

"Is something wrong?" I asked, suddenly afraid that John had somehow insulted her.

"That pounding outside is driving me *crazy.*"

"I'm really sorry," I said. "I'll try my hardest to do something about it."

"That would be thoughtful," she said in her Broadway-British voice. She continued with, "I was on the phone to Paris, and could barely *hear.* I have several more important calls to make."

"I'll definitely speak to Grover," I said, practically reeling out of her room.

"There's one other thing," Bette said with exasperation. "Your friend *Grace* called while you were out. She said something about coming over at one o'clock today. But I told her that that would be impossible since you and I would be having lunch *out*. I thought we'd lunch at Pierre's."

"I love Pierre's!"

"Good. It will be for just we girls," Bette said, terminating all discussion.

A lunch? For just "we girls"? It would be Jezebel and I, bent over a red checkered tablecloth, fresh-cut flowers and a bottle of bordeaux. For some unknown reason I suddenly had a vivid recollection of a childhood scene with my friend Cherry Preuss.

We were in her basement playing dress-up. Cherry grabbed all the good clothes and tossed me a wool army blanket and an old rope. "I'll be the movie star," she said, sliding her baby fat into one of her mother's battered evening dresses. "And you be the old shriveled nun."

I would have given my life to have Cherry Preuss walk into Pierre's and see the company I was now keeping. My reverie was suddenly interrupted with the reality that I had to tell Grover to put a silencer on his saw. Grover did not take the news in stride.

"Does the Power Princess want to finance sound-proofing her room?" he asked, digging a thumb into his tool belt.

"Maybe you could just do the quiet stuff until she leaves?" I asked.

"Quiet stuff? Like sending out the bill?" Grover said.

"Grover, we are talking about *Bette Davis*."

"Excuse me, Mrs. Fuller," Skipper said, seconds before he ran a two-by-four through the table saw. "That's not Bette Davis, the famous movie actress?"

"Didn't Grover tell you?"

"Nope," Grover said, brushing sawdust off his sleeves. "And I didn't tell him how she lit a match on the underside of my kitchen table, either."

"I saw her do that in one of her old movies," Skipper said. "I'll be gol-darn!" I could see the stars in his eyes. But at the time I didn't know just how star struck he was.

Grover and I bickered for twenty minutes before we came to a compromise. Grover and Skipper would arrive the next morning at ten o'clock instead of eight o'clock. And they would leave at six-thirty instead of four-thirty. That would give Bette two extra hours of quiet in the morning. In addition, I had arranged to pick up Christopher at preschool at four-thirty instead of the usual two-thirty, just in case Bette and I lingered over lunch.

We arrived at Pierre's at noon. Our entrance did not go unnoticed. Pierre himself greeted us, gave a modest bow, and whisked us to a cozy table beside a country brick fireplace. I overheard a few whispers from nearby tables. Unfortunately there wasn't a soul in the restaurant whom I knew.

The moment we sat down, Bette swept up a cigarette and her napkin in one dramatic move. Although I never smoked, I craved a cigarette with her every barbaric drag.

"Robin mentioned that this is one of your favorite restaurants," I said, groping for conversation.

"There are not many places with charm," she snapped. "Charm is such a *rarrre* commodity."

"I find that to be true," I said, thinking that

it was only a matter of time before the Tragedy Queen of the Warner Lot poured her heart out to me. Somehow I couldn't shake the feeling that Bette Davis chose to stay at my house because she sensed that I was a warm, caring person. And that *I* was someone who could understand her pain.

Bette ordered a white wine spritzer. "Make it two," I said to the waiter. Then she ordered Clams Casino for an appetizer.

"Don't put any garlic on those clams for god-sakes!" Bette commanded. "What a way to ruin good clams."

"I agree," I said. I, too, instructed the waiter to hold the garlic on my clams.

When the clams arrived, Bette poked at them with her fork. Then she mashed out her cigarette and proceeded to down the cherrystones one by one, as if consumed by an inward fire.

"These are delicious," I said in an attempt to break the awkward silence.

"The clams in *Maine* are delicious," she said.

"They're the best," I said. "Maine lobsters are the best, too," I added.

"Now you're talking," Bette said with inexhaust-ible vitality. "There's *nothing* better than a Maine lobster. We'll have some for this weekend."

This weekend? It was only Tuesday. According to my calculations, she was due to leave Thursday.

As I ate my clams, I began to plot how I would ever break this news to John. It was not going to be a pretty scene. But John was not my major concern. Bette was. I now felt certain that *I* was the reason she extended her visit. She related to my natural, no-nonsense style. *I* was someone she could feel comfortable with.

It wouldn't be long now before she would spill out her painful, ugly past to me. I reminded myself, however, that I could not initiate any such discussion. Just like a shrink, I would remain an active listener. No matter how close we became, I could never be judgmental.

Bette ordered the Casserole de Coquilles Saint Jacques, which consisted of bay scallops and mushrooms in a red wine and tarragon sauce. Once again I told the waiter, "Make it two."

"Young man," Bette said to the waiter, "I hope those scallops are not going to be swimming around in soggy sauce."

"Miss Davis," the waiter said, "I shall speak very sharply to the chef."

Bette took a sip of her wine spritzer and said, "I have had the most *dreadful* year with cooks. I have hired and fired dozens! I caught one cook red-handed serving me a dish that smacked of a frozen dinner. I confronted him with the Stouffers wrapping that he stupidly left in the trash. He was *out* the next day. It is impossible to get good help anymore!"

"Yes," I agreed, although the only cook that ever came into my kitchen was via cable TV.

The scallops were done to perfection. Pierre came over to ask how we were enjoying them. "They are quite tasty," Bette told Pierre agreeably.

Pierre's face lit up. "And Miss Davis," he said, "are you back in Westport to live? Or just on a visit?"

Pierre was as attractive as his accent. Bette looked at him like the brazen flirt she played in *Cabin in the Cotton* and said, "Just visiting."

God, how I loved her style. Her flair. Her bitchiness. She squeezed more out of two words than Shakespeare did out of five acts.

Pierre, friendly but formal, asked, "Can we look forward to seeing you in a new movie?"

"I'm waiting to do a film in Italy," she said, fluffing out the sides of her rather sparse strawberry blond hair. I half expected her to use her own campy line, "Ah'd love t' kiss ya, but ah jes washed mah hayuh."

"Now there's an attractive man," Bette said as Pierre walked away. "It's so hard to find an attractive, strong man. Gawd, the world is loaded with spineless sissies! If I ever find another man, he'll have to be as strong as I am!"

Here was my opening. I seized on it. "I'm sure you'll find what you're looking for soon," I said.

"*Christ*, who said I was looking for anything! I've never depended on *anyone* for *anything*, ever. The only person I've ever depended on was *myself*!"

This time I merely nodded as Bette went on venting: "The last time I saw B. D. she read to me from the Bible. 'Mother,' she said, 'unless you admit you're a sinner and turn your life over to Jesus, you will burn in hell!' *Brother*, if her sort is going to be in heaven, I'll take hell, thank you.

"Christ, I believe in God. I pray. I prayed like hell this past year. But prayer didn't get me out of that goddam hospital. I did it on my own. Me, myself! And my beautiful secretary, Kathryn. She was with me the *entire* time, encouraging me on those days when I was ready to throw in the towel."

"But now you're back in perfect shape," I said, aware that all the nearby patrons were straining their ears.

"Who said I'm perfect? Look at this goddam hand," she said, dangling a thin wrist festooned with gold. "It's like jelly. You call that perfect?" Then without even taking a beat, she shifted gears: "Darling, let's have a wonderful gooey chocolate dessert with our coffee."

"I'll have your Terrine de Chocolat Avec Marrons," Bette told the waiter. "And it had better be nice and chocolate-y."

"Make it two," I said.

Over dessert I brought up a subject I definitely had not planned. But my inner voice told me that it was time to help Bette see that there is so much more to life than stretch limos, screen credits, and Academy Awards. I thought, perhaps if I could help her to realize that she had a spiritual side, she could toss off the tinseled bondage of Hollywood and find an inner peace. On the other hand, Hollywood and its artifices were never exactly repellent to me. As a kid I couldn't wait to get out of Cleveland Heights, move to Hollywood, and break into the movies where I would be flooded in money, jewels, Cadillacs, and gaudy homes.

I took a couple of bites of the rich chocolate cake to fortify myself and then blurted out: "Fifteen years ago I discovered quite by accident that I was actually psychic."

"Christ!" Bette said. "Ruthie was psychic too."

"She was?" I asked.

"It was Ruthie who predicted my success," Bette said, sinking her cigarette into what was left of her dessert. "I was doing the play, *Broadway*. I had a minor part. My mother told me that I *must* learn the part of the girl who falls down the stairs. She was *adamant* that I learn that part. I did as Ruthie said. Sure enough, one evening something happened and the girl couldn't go on. I took her place. The reviews were *smashing*. And that was the beginning!"

"Did your mother ever predict anything else?" I asked.

"*Thousands* of things!" Bette said. "One summer in Maine, Robin and I had been at a dance at a place where they had big bands. I was dancing my heart out. All of a sudden I looked up, and there was Ruthie. Brother, was I thrilled to see her," Bette said as she adjusted a cuff on her white silk shirt. "Ruthie told me that I *must* come right home. She had an omen that the boy I was with was going to have a car accident. Ruthie was right. That night he had an accident."

I captured Bette's undivided attention when I told her about a strange but true story that John had written and I had helped research called "The Ghost of Flight 401." It was the story of an Eastern Airlines jet that crashed into the Everglades back in 1972. A short time later, crew members reported seeing the full-bodied apparition of the flight engineer, who had been killed in the crash. I told Bette it was during the course of that research that I discovered I had psychic ability. I found myself revealing factual information about details of the deceased flight engineer's life that I could not possibly have learned by ordinary means.

"So you, Ruthie, and Shirley MacLaine have a lot in common," Bette said with more than a touch of sarcasm. Then she added, "I shall pay this bill and we'll be on our way."

Not content to drop the psychic stuff, I went for broke. "If you like, after dinner tonight we could try to maybe contact Ruthie on the Other Side."

Bette dropped her alligator wallet onto the table and stared at me as if I were a stark raving lunatic. Then she spat out, "For chrissakes, Ruthie was a pain in the ass when she was alive. I can't imagine what she's like on the Other Side!"

The moment I cleaned up the dinner dishes, Bette and I went into the living room to relax by the fire—although John claimed that you couldn't use the words *relax* and *Bette* in the same sentence. John excused himself on the pretense of catching up on the writing of his tornado book.

"Well, ladies," he said, "I guess I'll bury myself in a cumulonimbus cloud."

"I'd rather be buried in that than in the hallelujah of evangelists or the cacophony of saws and hammers!"

"Speaking of evangelists," John said as he climbed the stairs to his office, "Grace called while you were at Pierre's this afternoon. She says she has something urgent to talk to you about."

Once again, I could count on John to press all of Bette's buttons.

"What's she got—a new shipment of Jesus pinky

rings?" Bette asked in her deadpan diction.

"I've got a good idea," I said. "Why don't I get out the Ouija board."

Bette shot a glare at me as if I should be taken to my room for shock treatment. But then she said mockingly, "Yes, let's see what Ruthie's up to."

I got out the Ouija board and rested it on my lap.

"Ruthie," I said with my eyes momentarily closed, "could you please come through with a message for Bette?"

"Yes, Ruthie," Bette said in her little girl voice, "where the hell are you?"

My fingers were resting on the plastic indicator. Suddenly the indicator began to move across the alphabet in a wide circle. Then it spelled out the word NEAR.

"She says she's near," I said to Bette, who was now pacing the living room, her cigarette in perpetual motion.

"Ruthie, if you are near," Bette said in her dramatic, choppy speech, "why can't I see you?"

The Ouija pointer spelled out: I AM IN A DIFFERENT DIMENSION.

"Is it like 3-D, Ruthie?" Bette asked, stabbing out a fresh cigarette and giving a mirthless chuckle.

The answer came quickly: WAIT YOU WILL SEE.

"Jesus, Ruthie, cut the shit!" Bette said, throwing her head to the ceiling. "I wish to hell you were here to read B. D.'s *charming* book. What a *splennndid* piece of fiction that is!"

The indicator spelled out: SHE IS AS HEADSTRONG AS YOU.

"Brother!" Bette said, lobbing a lighted cigarette into the fireplace. "Ruthie hasn't changed a bit over there. Or wherever the hell she is!"

"Bette," I asked, "do you think we should ask Ruthie about Joan? You know, Crawford?"

"Jesus, I *beg* of you, don't bring up that dame's name," Bette pleaded as she struck a match on the underside of our coffee table.

"I'm sorry," I said. "But you know, maybe Joan has changed now that she's passed over."

"What in the hell are you talking about 'passing over'? She is *dead*. Capital D-E-A-D, *dead!*"

"But you know," I said to Bette, "she is still 'over there.' There's no other place for her to be."

"Well if she's 'over there' ask her what she's doing for disinfectant and rubber gloves," Bette said, overemphasizing each word.

At this point Bette went into a monologue about Joan.

"Every time that neurotic bitch went into a hotel room she got down on her hands and knees and scrubbed the bathroom floor. Christ, if she hadn't spent her whole life whoring around, she wouldn't have had that sanitation hang-up. She even had her *walls* covered in plastic. *Nevvvver* would she touch anybody's hands . . ."

After a polite length of time, I reminded Bette that we had to be serious if we wanted to receive psychic messages.

She ignored me. "Ask Miss Crawford," Bette said, "if she knows my daughter did me in *too*. At least Ms. Crawford's daughter waited until she went 'over there.' "

The Ouija board indicator began to move. Then it slowed and stopped. "Nothing seems to be coming through on that one," I told Bette.

Bette ignored me again. "Ask Ms. Crawford if she knows that I'm still going strong."

Still the indicator did not move. "It's not moving," I said.

"You're goddam right. She hasn't changed a bit 'over there.' Still as jealous as hell! Every time I think of all those gifts she sent me that I *immediately* returned, I want to *vaahmit*! Black stiletto heels. Come-fuck-me pumps! The bitch was nothing but a second-rate prostitute . . ."

I asked Bette, "Is there anyone else you might want to contact?"

"Yes, that goddam publisher about my book. I've been slaving day and night over it."

"Is the publisher dead?" I asked.

"He may as well be!" Bette said, snapping another lit cigarette into the fireplace.

"We can talk only to the dead," I said to Bette, "not the living." Then I added, "Should we ask your mother if she's seen your father?"

"Jesus," Bette said, twirling a freshly lit cigarette, "he didn't want to see Ruthie when he was alive. Why the *hell* would they want to be together when they're both *dead*?"

"I don't know," I said. "Maybe we can find out?"

"Ruthie," Bette said, ignoring my suggestion, "if you happen to bump into Ms. Crawford, do ask her what she's doing for falsies up there!" Bette roared with laughter.

I asked Bette: "Is there one final question for Ruthie?"

"Yes, ask Ruthie if I'll ever get another decent part? I've been sent nothing but *crap*. If Aaron Spelling sends me one more lousy script for that shit series "Hotel," I'll curl up and die!"

The indicator spelled out: NEXT YEAR.

"Well, at least Ruthie is counting on me being 'down here' for another year anyway!" Bette said in a cloud of smoke. She sounded quite triumphant. She also sounded as if she didn't for one moment believe Ruthie had come through.

"Darling," Bette said to me as I packed up the Ouija board, "I'll need to have the house quiet tomorrow. I intend to work all day on my book."

"No problem," I said. "The carpenters won't be here till ten o'clock tomorrow morning. And they'll be working on the other side of the house."

"Thank *Gawd* for small favors!" she said, slamming the door behind her.

Then it struck me: Grace was to arrive early in the morning for an all-day interview that was critical for me to meet the deadline of my book about her.

I was caught between the jaws of the sacred and the profane. I didn't have the nerve even to tell Bette about my scheduled interview with Grace.

I didn't sleep for five minutes that night.

3

STORM CENTER

At nine-thirty the next morning, when I heard no sign of Bette stirring, I gently but firmly knocked on her door. "Miss Davis," I whispered, "would you like me to bring you a cup of hot coffee?"

"*Kee-ryst*! I don't want you to bring me *cold* coffee," she gurgled. Then she whipped the door open.

I literally jumped back, startled and repelled. Her blue eyes were bulging through a thick layer of cold cream that made her look like Baby Jane in the scene where she kicked Crawford down a flight of stairs.

"Did you sleep all right?" I asked, trying to sweeten the atmosphere.

"Not a goddam wink! I lay awake on that trampoline you call a bed, *dreading* the arrival of those two Neanderthals."

"You mean Skipper and Grover?"

"Well I don't mean Peck and Cagney!"

"I'm afraid that they're due here in about half an hour," I said, trying to get up my nerve to tell her that Grace, of all people, was also due any moment.

"Isn't that just *ducky*," she said, whisking past me to the kitchen.

"How about if I fix you a soft-boiled egg to go with your Carnation Instant Breakfast drink?" I asked as I obsequiously followed the barefooted Empress of Burbank to the kitchen. Robin had told me that she "adored" soft-boiled eggs in the morning.

"No eggs today, darling," Bette said so affably that I actually felt my heart quicken. John probably would have said that I was experiencing arrhythmia—a heart condition brought on by nervous exhaustion.

"I bought the cutest little egg cups at a church tag sale," I said, sounding suspiciously like June Cleaver.

Bette made no verbal comment. Her eyes, however, said, "Gawd, save me from this mental defective!"

"Can I get you anything special at the store today?" I asked, in a weak effort to get back on her good side.

"*Pleeeze* get some decent cookies. If I eat one more of those Oreos, I'll curl up and die. Pepperidge Farm makes a good cookie."

"I'll go right now," I said, sliding an ashtray under her cigarette that was about to incinerate the butcher-block counter.

"That's kind of you," Bette said, mixing the Carnation drink into Christopher's Mickey Mouse cup.

Then just as Bette took the first sip of her instant breakfast, Grace's mission van pulled into our driveway.

"Oh no," I said feigning surprise. "I'm afraid Grace is here."

"*Brother*," Bette snarled as she headed to her room. She had a cigarette in one hand and the Mickey Mouse cup in the other. "If God is so good," she muttered, "why the hell doesn't he spare me the pulpit pounders?"

There was a moment of silence before Grace burst through the front door shouting: "Hallelujah!"

"Hi, Grace," I said as softly as possible.

"Well praise God!" Grace said with boundless enthusiasm. "I've got very, very important news for Bette Davis."

Against my better judgment, I knocked on Bette's door.

"Who's there?" Bette barked.

"It's only me, Miss Davis," I said, adding, "may I come in for a quick moment?"

"Are you alone?"

"Yes I am," I choked.

"Come in!"

Bette was seated at our ancient Goodwill store desk that was minus a couple of side drawers. The cold cream was now off her face, and she was smearing on lipstick and looking into a handheld mirror.

"You know Grace is in the other room," I said. Then I steeled myself against being ground down to a fine dust and blown away.

"That's precisely why I'm in *this* room!" Bette snapped, dropping the mirror to her lap.

"Well, I can really appreciate how you feel about Grace," I said, "but she claims to have something very, very important to tell you."

"And you can tell your evangelist that I have something very, very important to tell *her*," Bette said as she blotted her Lancôme lips with a tissue— a tissue I was tempted to save and later frame.

"What's that?" I asked.

"*Balls!*" she exploded.

"I'll pass that message along," I answered as I backed away from this ninety-pound larger-than-life character.

When Grace finally realized that she wasn't going to have an audience with Bette Davis, she told me what the "very, very important message" was: Grace's friend had seen Bette's daughter, B. D., on the Christian TV show "The 700 Club." On the show, B. D. told the host that she was sorry for having ever written the book about her famous mother.

I immediately passed this information along to Bette. As I spoke, Bette bugged her partially made-up eyes and raised her eyebrows practically to the hairline. Then just as suddenly her eyes retreated and her face dropped to settle into deep grooves and valleys. She had a thousand-mile stare. Deadly quiet descended over the room. Uncomfortable with the quiet curtain, I turned to leave.

"I want to see a tape of that show," Bette ordered from her Goodwill command post.

"I'll ask Grace if she can get one," I said.

"Elizabeth," Bette said with full animation returned, "that will be *most* important!"

I nodded. I knew what she meant. If B. D. was truly sorry she wrote that book then Bette would be willing to forgive her only biological child the anguish she caused and they could be together once again. Bette, however, never would have verbalized that to me.

Grace didn't see any problem in getting a tape of the TV show. In fact the very next day Grace brought over the tape. Bette stayed in her room, but she sent a message through me to thank Grace. Grace was disappointed that Bette didn't personally thank her for all of her trouble, not to mention the expense of Federal Express overnight delivery.

That afternoon, Bette, John, and I watched the tape. The interviewer opened the program by showing old movie photos of Bette Davis. "At this very moment," the host began, "the First Lady of the American Screen might actually be watching this show . . ."

I did a double take on that one. Bette was sure as hell watching the show with us in our bedroom, although in delayed form on our VCR. I looked around the room. The TV set was perched precariously on a shaky cabinet at the foot of our bed, where John was sprawled. John seemed more intent on stuffing his pipe with Captain Black than admiring the montage of glamour portraits shown on the screen.

Bette and I were seated on a little alcove seat framed out of barn wood at the side of the room, leaning back on a pile of cushions. One of the pillows had a phrase printed across it: "I'd rather be forty than pregnant." That pillow did not escape those Bette Davis eyes. "Brother!" she bellowed, "I'd rather be ninety than pregnant!"

"Gee, Miss Davis," I said, pointing to the screen that suddenly flashed a still photo of her as Charlotte Vale in her Academy Award nomination, *Now, Voyager*. "I'll never forget the line when Charlotte turned to Jim and said: 'Oh, Jim, let's not ask for the moon. We have the stars.'"

"*Jim!*" Bette roared, yanking her frail frame to a stiff sitting position. "Who-the-fuck-is-*Jim*? It was *Jerry*! Charlotte looked up at *Jerry* and said: 'Oh, Jerry, don't let's ask for the moon. We have the stars.'"

"Yes," I said, coughing on the second-hand pipe and cigarette smoke. "That line sounds *exactly* like it did in the movie—"

"For *chrissake*, it damn well should!" she blasted, as she viciously crushed out her cigarette in Christopher's pewter porridge bowl. "Who the hell do you think played Charlotte Vale!"

With that verbal punch delivered in classic Bette Davis style, she slipped on a pair of black-framed glasses, scooped up her Bic lighter, lit another cigarette, and then leaned forward to take in every word of the commentator:

"Now a memoir has been written by Bette Davis's only natural child, B. D. Hyman," the host said. "Barbara Davis has revealed a side of family life in *My Mother's Keeper* that has created a minor storm in Hollywood—"

"That naughty little girl has revealed a side of a fantasy family smack out of Charles Addams!" Bette snapped as she drew in an inhuman drag.

"I just finished reading your book," the host said as he swiveled his chair to suddenly reveal B. D., the thirty-eight-year-old daughter of the famous star. "I'm exhausted after reading it. But you actually lived it."

B. D. chuckled.

"What inspired you to write this?" the host probed.

"What inspired me was the effort to get through to my mother . . ."

I looked out of the corner of my eye toward Bette. Her eyes were fixed on the screen. Her stone face matched the whole array on Mount Rushmore.

B. D. went on: "I wanted my mother to know that there is kindness and goodness. One doesn't have to fight and compete for love. You see, to my mother, love and ownership are synonymous—"

"Your mother," the host interrupted, "could be watching this show right now, right?"

"Possibly," B. D. said. "I hope she is. I hope she watches what I say. And I hope it increases her desire to understand what I've said in my book—"

"Well, my darling little girl," Bette said to our TV screen, "it increases my desire to choke the life out of you!"

"Do you feel in any way that you've dishonored her?" the host asked in a tone that was smothered in marshmallow whip.

"No," B. D. said matter-of-factly. "I suppose some people see it that way . . ."

"B. D.," the host said, "for those who haven't read the book, there's violence, there's manipulation. There is darkness. It's a lurid story. Jealousy. There aren't enough adjectives to describe all of this."

"Balls!" Bette said with her cigarette clamped between her forefinger and thumb in vintage Bette Davis. "I wonder when my little darling is going to admit that she manufactured all of those Dickensian stories for that big fat advance. She was counting on me being *dayead* by publication date. Christ, I already had three strokes. Nobody thought I'd make it. Nobody except Kathryn and me. *Weeeee* knew it all along . . ."

Although Bette's tongue spit acid, her eyes were moist. It was not a Bette Davis I had ever seen before. I sensed her hurt. Her humiliation. Her loss of dignity.

John and I were embarrassed to be watching the show. We felt like intruders. We got up to leave. However, Bette called us back. "*Jeeesus*! don't leave me here to suffer this crap alone!"

"When you were younger," the host asked B. D., "when did you realize that there was a real problem?"

"Mother and I got along well when I was a child," B. D. said. "I loved her. I still do love her. And she loved me. We had a lot of good times together—"

"Oh my, B. D.," Bette said to the ceiling. "That confession is *not* going to help sell your book!"

Earlier in the day Bette had left a small black booklet on the kitchen table. I peeked inside. It had telephone numbers. On the back pages the ages and sizes of all of her grandchildren were meticulously recorded. Next to each child's name was written in her own handwriting the child's favorite colors and toys.

Back on the TV screen the host asked: "Your mother's been married four times?"

"That's right," Bette quipped. "Each time it got worse!"

The interviewer continued with: "Have you been able to come to any conclusions on why your mother is *so* insecure?"

"I don't know what drives her," B. D. said. "I think she has personal demons—"

"*Jesus!*" Bette wailed, "these born-again Christians are *obsessed* with demons!"

"I don't think mother is demon-possessed," B. D. said to the host.

"Well-*thank*-you-Barbara-Davis!" Bette said, curt and clipped.

Then B. D. said, "But I think she has these forces that work within her. She has a very negative view of the world. She feels she has to fight the whole world every minute of every day, and she can never let down her guard and just be—"

"*Shee-yit!*" Bette roared. "The minute you let your guard down the Crawfords of this world are ready to rip-the-*guts*-out of you! Every time Crawford got near me I could feel her trying to *annihilate* me! She *hay-ayted* being Number Two. The only thing I regret is that I didn't get to slap her around more in *Baby Jane*. Whenever a scene called for me to belt her she had Aldrich bring in her double. Christ, I knew how to clip her without hurting her. Crawford was *no* pro! When we shot the scene where I had to carry her from the bed into the hallway, the bitch weighted herself down with a lead belt! I almost broke my fucking back. Worse, in the scene where the old broad was croaking on the beach, she strapped on a pair of falsies that made her look like the Hollywood Hills. Can you imagine a pair of giant tits jutting up toward the sky on someone who for the last twenty years was supposed to have been wasting away? During the scene that called for me to fall on top of her, the breath was knocked out of me. Christ, the bitch wrecked my back and my front . . ."

Again, our attention shifted back to the TV screen. "Have you told your mother about God?" the interviewer asked B. D.

"Oh yes," B. D. said. "I read her the six scriptural steps to salvation. The first step being Acknowledge, for all have sinned and fallen short of the glory of God. Mother became outraged. She would scream: 'I have never committed a sin! No one is ever going to make me say that. Not even your god!' "

At this point, the host asked that everyone watching the show pray for Bette Davis, Queen of the Silver Screen, to accept the Lord Jesus Christ into her life.

The "Queen" did not take this sitting on our barn wood throne. "Brother!" she said, pacing six inches from the TV screen. "I wonder how many 'saints' out there are writing checks to that holier-than-thou TV fop!"

"Enough to keep that fruit whip in shiny suits and stretch limos," John interjected from the bed.

"Now you're talking!" Bette said, giving a full-bodied roar that only encouraged John to come up with more one-liners aimed at TV evangelists.

"I bet he moonlights for Dial-a-Desire," John said, pausing for the laugh.

I had to hand it to John. He was brilliant, funny, and a royal pain in the ass. With a few clever jokes he had *my* idol suddenly finding him *très charmant*. Bette had been in our house for a full five days, and not once did she even crack a smile at anything I said. Come to think of it, she didn't even appear to be listening to anything I said.

The evening before at dinner, I told Bette about how I had once worn my mother out looking for a red dress just like the one she wore in *Jezebel* for my high school prom. I told her about how I plastered bright red lipstick on my lips, and how my grandmother and I used to subscribe to all the movie magazines in hopes of learning everything we could about her. I even told her about the time I had brought my Bette Davis collection of fan magazine photos to school. I had been in the girls' room showing them to my friends when all of a sudden Sister Mary Agnes appeared. She grabbed the photos and ripped them to shreds. Later she gave me a stack of holy cards and told me to pray to Saint Jude, patron of hopeless causes.

After I poured out my heart, a pathetic smile emerged through the thick lipstick of this Living Legend. "So," she said with her bulging eyes at half mast, "I think I shall collapse early tonight."

I felt like a real fool. Our "bonding" was going very, very slowly. But I reassured myself that life-long relationships were not built on the ability to come up with jokes. Personally, I always felt that telling jokes was a way to avoid communicating. John may have had her temporary interest, but it was shallow and superficial. I was confident, however, that in a few short days Bette Davis would see that *I* was a deep person, with unlimited vision and insight. *I* was indeed someone who could help her see that life need not be a painful struggle. *I* could show her how to find a richer meaning in her life. She need not live off her nervous energy. Perhaps I could teach her how to meditate. But whatever I did, I couldn't rush her into anything.

As the TV interview drew to an end, Bette was anxiously waiting for her daughter to express remorse for having written the tell-all book. Although Bette didn't come out and admit that, I could read it in her gestures. Each time the host asked B. D. a question, Bette would jut forward so as to not miss a word of her daughter's response.

"Why should anyone believe your side of the story?" the interviewer asked B. D.

"I know it's the truth," B. D. said without hesitation. "And lots of people in the book who were part of things that went on, wrote to me to say that it was true. It was like being there."

Again the host probed, "B. D., do you love your mother?"

The answer came fast: "Yes I do. I wouldn't be doing this if I didn't love her."

"What a strange way of showing your love, daughter," Bette said, wringing her pipe-cleaner-thin fingers. Then she leaned back and added, "She's-a-*handsome*-specimen! There's *nothinnng* that woman can't do well."

Finally the tortuous interview ended. B. D. never even came close to saying that she was sorry for having written the book. Grace had been misinformed—a fact Bette surprisingly let slip by without comment.

"Elizabeth," Bette said, smashing her cigarette into Christopher's Fisher-Price tow truck, "I hope to *gawd* your offspring never sticks it to you the way mine did!" Then she turned to John, who was eyeballing the truck, and added in her best Margo Channing diction: "Life-isn't-for-sissies!"

At that moment, I had an impulsive desire to wrap my arms around her delicate shoulders and hug her. I wanted to tell her that as a mother I could understand her heartache. I wanted to tell Bette that I understood not only her pain but B. D.'s pain as well. But of course I said none of the above. The time was not right.

John headed back to his studio office. Bette and I headed downstairs to the kitchen for a cup of tea to go with the Pepperidge Farm cookies.

As luck would have it, Grover and Skipper were planted at the kitchen bar having one of their too frequent breaks. To make matters worse, they were helping themselves to the cookies earmarked for Bette Davis.

"I see you guys found the cookies," I said to Grover, who was talking on the phone.

"Christ, how long has he been on that phone?" Bette asked as she snatched a handful of cookies out of the box. "Italy is ringing me this afternoon!"

"They already rang," Grover said, covering the mouthpiece of the phone.

"Italy called!" Bette belted.

"About twenty minutes ago," Grover said in his down-east accent. "I had to put Stubby from the lumberyard on hold while I fielded your call."

"Jesus!" Bette snapped. "I've been waiting for two days for that call to come through." Her eyes were once again on fire with the prospect of shooting her film.

"And I've been waiting six lousy days for two French doors to be delivered!" Grover said with a huff, nodding toward Skipper for his approval.

Skipper just sat at the bar in a boneless sort of way. His eyes followed Bette all around the kitchen.

"I'm afraid all of this is my fault," I apologized. "I did tell Grover not to disturb us for any reason."

"If it's important they'll call back," Grover said as he hung up and then immediately dialed another number.

"How the *hell* am I going to get my calls through if he spends all day on the goddam phone?" Bette said, fixing herself a wine spritzer.

"Not to worry," Grover reassured Bette. "We've got Totalphone here. You can hear a beep if somebody's trying to get through."

"Miss Davis," Skipper said, "I sure would appreciate your autograph."

"Elizabeth," Bette said, blatantly ignoring Skipper's request, "I'm sure you have important things to do this afternoon, just as I do!"

"As a matter of fact, I do have to catch up on writing my book," I said, careful not to mention Grace's name.

"And *I* must work on *my* book, too," Bette said, taking a verbal swipe at Grover and Skipper, who were still lounging at the kitchen bar. Then she plucked up the box of Pepperidge Farm cookies and left the room, slamming the door behind her.

Less than thirty seconds later she was back.

"Kee-ryst!" she screeched, "what *moron* moved my desk out onto that deck! Squirrels and birds have crapped on my manuscript!"

"That's just caulking," Grover said. "From Harold's caulking gun."

"Jeeesus, Grover!" I said, throwing my shoulders back and planting my hands on my hips, Bette Davis style. "Why the *hell* didn't you tell us you were moving Miss Davis's desk?"

"Not to worry," Grover said, cool and collected. "Harold's on his way back now with the new sliding glass door. Everything will be put back in its place in less than an hour."

"Isn't that just *ducky*!" I said.

Bette was thoroughly enjoying every moment of the tiff.

"Really give it to him!" she muttered, plunging her fist forward like a coach.

To keep Bette in high spirits, I continued to blast Grover. As I did, I flailed my arms, swayed my hips, and bulged my eyes, or at least that's what Grover later accused me of doing. But at the time the only thing I was consciously aware of was that the more I laid into Grover, the more Bette enjoyed the scene.

I could see now that Bette and I were well on our way to bonding. All of this of course was at poor Grover's expense. Later I would make it up to Grover. I would keep the refrigerator well stocked with prune Danish and brownies.

After I finished my tirade of abuse, Grover asked, "Are you through?" On the surface he was still cool and collected, but underneath I could see that he was ready to explode.

"I-am-quite-through!" I snapped, borrowing Bette's clipped tongue.

I nodded toward Bette. Her eyes were sparkling like Christmas tree ornaments. I was deliriously happy. I was practically Bette Davis's best friend!

4

FRONT-PAGE WOMAN

At the beginning of the second week, Bette had settled in. She had taken over the guest closet, linen closet, and our "junk" closet with her accessories: Italian shoes, designer clothes, and French hats. John complained that the bathroom vanity looked like a makeup room at Twentieth Century Fox. And he really squawked the morning he was forced to use Bette's bathroom because our own bathroom was under repair.

"She had the *gall* to move my shaving gear out of the medicine chest to make room for her inventory of pastel lotion and crap!"

"I told her she could move your stuff." I was lying now, defending my new "best friend."

"Liz!" John wailed, "that Czar of Celluloid is taking over our house!" John spoke loud enough for Grover to comment.

"I'll drink to that!" Grover called to us from our bathroom where he was ripping up mildewed floorboards.

"Lower your voices, you guys," I said. "She might hear."

John jumped in to say, "It wouldn't matter to her, even if she did hear."

"She can't hear," Grover called from the distance. "She's on the phone to Paris, France."

"How do you know *that*?" I asked. "And why in the hell do you have to say 'Paris, *France*!' "

"I heard her place the call," Grover said, ignoring my outburst. "These old walls are as thin as tracing paper."

"She'd better be putting that call on her credit card," John said.

"She didn't," Grover said.

"Liz," John said with a sudden look of panic, "did she mention anything about paying for these calls?"

"Of course she did," I lied again. "She told me just yesterday that she was keeping track of every penny. She's going to reimburse us when she leaves."

"Who's paying for the lobster she wants tonight?" Grover asked.

Grover undoubtedly had overheard Bette and me discussing the dinner menu—the way Grover overheard everything else.

"Lobster?" John said.

"Aren't lobsters going for $6.99 a pound this time of year?" Grover said. Then he tossed old floorboards out the bathroom window.

"You should know, Grover," I snapped. "You

seem to have a handle on everything!"

"Who's paying for the lobsters?" John pressed on.

"I refuse to get snagged into this petty conversation," I said. "You still don't seem to appreciate the fact that we are housing the *most* important film star in the *world!* Do you know that she's even bigger in England than she is here?"

"So was Bloody Mary," John said, pleased with himself.

I could hear Grover snickering.

"I wasn't going to tell you this," I said to John. "But yesterday when Bette and I were driving home from Peter's Market, she suddenly blurted out: 'Elizabeth-tell-me-about-your-psychic-prowess.' "

"And?" John said.

"And I told her all about it. Seances and all."

Grover gave another snicker.

"What's your point, Liz?" John asked.

"My point is that this was the very *first* time that she had ever asked me a question."

"*So?*" John said, as he slipped on a pair of khaki shorts.

"So she's interested in learning about the non-material world," I said. "You see, Bette Davis is staying in our house and she doesn't even know why."

"Liz," John said, condescending, "she's simply camping here till the hotel strike is over—or her movie comes through in Italy. Don't read anything exalted into it."

"On a conscious level she believes that she's here for those reasons," I explained, "but her higher self has directed her here to *me* so that I can help her realize her spiritual nature. Her spiritual self is crying out to be nourished."

"You've been smoking something, Liz," John said.

"And I've got something else to tell you," I said. "Tonight after I put Christopher to bed, Bette, you, and I are going to have a seance."

"A what?" John asked.

"You heard me. A seance. I told Bette that it was nothing spooky."

"Did she agree to this?" John wanted to know.

"More or less," I said. "I've got her intrigued about the whole idea."

"Well you can leave me out of this," John said.

"You've *got* to be part of it," I pleaded. "Bette was really curious to know how *you* felt about seances. I made a real point of telling her that you believe in spirit communication. It seemed to impress her that a tough-minded journalist would buy the idea of a seance," I said, flattering John into going along with it.

Later that afternoon, I got out of the car with Bette and Christopher at Compo Beach. As I did, I wondered why on earth I had ever suggested we go to the beach. Christopher alone was a handful. But I knew Bette didn't want to be stuck home with Skipper and Grover repairing the roof just above her bedroom. Bette especially didn't want to be anywhere near Skipper and his conspicuous flirting.

Two days earlier, Bette had found a "poem" slipped under her door. In scribbled handwriting it read:

Dear Betty:
I see the moon I see the stars but
no star shines as brite as you.
You are heaven to me.
Love, Skipper

This "sonnet" did not exactly evoke a warm and fuzzy feeling inside Bette. She crushed the yellow foolscap in her fist and ground out between her teeth: "I can see the local carpenters' union is not ready to elect a poet laureate."

Bette had to lean her linguini-thin body against the wind as we started toward the beach. She was incognito in a large straw hat, sunglasses, white duck slacks, and *my* beach sandals. Christopher scooted ahead with his bucket and shovel, dragging a Superman towel behind him.

When we reached the edge of the beach, I offered Bette my arm as a support. She flicked it away, thundering: "I've walked on sand before! Who the hell do you think I am, Crawford? Christ, the beach scene in *Baby Jane* had to be shot on a special set inside the goddam studio. Aldrich had to bring in *tonnnns* of sand all because Miss Crawford had it written into her contract that at all times the temperature had to be an arctic fifty degrees. The neurotic bitch couldn't *staaaand* the heat, the sun, the sand . . ."

"She didn't look like the delicate sort to me," I interjected.

"*Delicate*!" Bette roared loud enough for a sunbathing mother to stop applying lotion to her child and look up. "Crawford was a *boozer*! If your body is saturated with booze you perspire in the heat.

Vodka was Crawford's life-support system!"

Cautiously Bette picked her way around the crowd to the edge of the water where Christopher had already joined a cluster of kids erecting a sand castle.

"Where would you like me to put the beach chairs?" I asked Bette.

"On the damn beach!" she said, clearly agitated over the long walk on the sand.

"Right," I said. I promptly put the cooler down and then unfolded her chair.

"I hope we're on the *smoking* side of the beach!" Bette said dryly as she expertly lit a cigarette in the breeze.

"Yeah," I said, "I hate those self-righteous people who have divided the world into smoking and non-smoking sections." The truth of the matter is, *I* was one of those do-gooders who felt smokers had no rights. But now I would sooner die from secondhand cigarette smoke than let Bette know my true feelings.

Once we were settled in our beach chairs, I handed Bette the *Daily News*. I scanned the *Times* book review section that I didn't get around to reading on Sunday. B. D.'s book was on the hardcover bestseller list. I didn't point that out to Bette. I didn't need to.

"Is it still on the bestselling list?" Bette asked, flipping pages looking for information on the hotel strike.

"Number seven," I said, barely audible.

"It'll go to number one," Bette said with a strange mixture of pride and disgust in her voice. "I've made my little girl a bestselling author. I do hope she appreciates that."

"Why do you think she wrote it?" I asked, aware that I was overstepping the boundary.

"Money. Money. Money." Bette said flatly.

"I finished reading it last night," I said.

I waited in suspense for Bette's response. It was minutes in coming.

"*Sooooo* you read the book?" Bette said. Her eyes did not leave the *Daily News*.

"Yes," I said. "I feel it's a very hurtful book."

"*Hurtful!*" she exploded. "It's *killlling* me! I loved that child more than anything I've ever loved in my life. B. D. lived a privileged life. I gave her *everything*! She was raised in the East. A good, solid Yankee upbringing. And *I* was always there for her. I was there for Michael and poor sweet Margot . . ."

Michael and Margot were adopted as infants by Bette and Gary Merrill. When Margot was only two years old they discovered that she was retarded. As a toddler she had unusual strength and was often destructive to herself as well as to Michael and B. D. Bette and Gary had to make the painful decision to send Margot to a special school that caters to brain-damaged children. Michael, however, was a bright child, and is now a successful lawyer in Boston. Bette seemed very proud of him.

Bette went on: "When B. D. was only sixteen she said she wanted to get married. I didn't think it was a good idea. But she was *most* convincing. I went along with it. I gave her a beautiful wedding. What a bride! The most beautiful bride in the world! For her honeymoon I made certain that black silk sheets were on their connubial couch. B. D.'s husband had a thing for black silk sheets," Bette said, rolling her eyes. "I honestly didn't think the marriage would last a year. But it did. I *nevvvver* thought my child would be capable of doing this to me. *Nevvvverrr!* Thank *Gawd* I've always had my work. *Work* is the only thing that won't let you down!"

Then Bette turned to me and abruptly changed gears. "Liz," she said, "would you mind bringing me some water. I need to take my pills."

Since I had only soft drinks in the cooler, I went to the sandwich shop, leaving Bette to look after Christopher. As I walked toward the shop, my mind swelled as much as the waves on the beach. I wanted to shout to everyone on the beach that I was hanging out with Bette Davis. And more than that, Bette Davis was wearing *my* beach sandals! God, if a psychic had ever told me twenty years ago that one day Bette Davis would be lounging at the beach with *me*, revealing intimate details of her life, baby-sitting *my* kid, taking *my* phone messages, I would have shredded her tarot cards.

Standing in the endless food line, I thought about an incident that happened earlier in the day. While I was having a shower Bette answered the phone, taking messages. Later, Bette reported that Grace called two times. Both times Grace said, "God bless you, Miss Davis," and both times Bette let her have it: "God already *has* blessed me!"

In addition to Grace calling, Christopher's pediatrician's office phoned. "First the nurse said, 'We need to change the time of Christopher's appointment from two o'clock to three o'clock!' " Bette said in her overblown style, adding, "Then she called right back and said, 'No, make it three-thirty.' And I told the nurse: 'Make up your goddam mind!' "

It took nearly fifteen minutes in line to get Bette's cup of water. Walking back to the beach, I prayed that Christopher was not bothering her again. On the drive to the beach, Christopher had managed to stand up in his car seat and threatened to dump the remnants of last week's sand out of the bucket and onto Bette's head. I nearly ran the car off the road trying to get the bucket out of his sticky little hands.

When I arrived back at our beach chairs, Bette and Christopher were not there. I thought that they had decided to have a little walk along the beach. I scanned the horizon. They were nowhere to be seen. Then I thought that perhaps Christopher had to use the restroom. I walked there, searching the beach as I did so. There was no Christopher or Bette in the restrooms.

It occurred to me that Christopher had probably talked Bette into taking him to the beach playground. But they weren't there either. Then I checked the sandwich shop, thinking that Christopher wanted french fries. They were not there.

Suddenly I heard Bette shouting Christopher's name. She was halfway between the sandwich shop and the water. I ran toward her.

"Where's Christopher?" I shouted. I was out of breath.

Bette picked up her black cane and pointed it toward a group of children. "One moment he was playing with those kids and the next he was gone," she said with a distinct nervous quiver to her voice.

"Maybe he's in the water!" I screeched. I ran along the edge of the water with macabre images of Christopher floating facedown.

"Has anybody seen a little boy with a red bathing suit!" I shouted to everybody within hearing range.

People suddenly rose from their chairs and towels and began searching with me.

"Somebody get a lifeguard!" shouted a husky man, dripping in oil. "A little boy's missing!"

"Oh my God," I shouted hysterically, thinking that if he hadn't drowned some pervert had snatched him up.

At that very moment a loud, clear voice blasted over the lifeguard's bullhorn: "Will 'Mommy' and Bette Davis please come to the lifeguard's station and pick up a boy named Christopher." At once the phrase was repeated. Then again and again.

"That's me!" I said, rushing up the beach toward the lifeguard's station.

"Are you 'Mommy'?" the lifeguard said. Christopher was on his lap. They were both smiling.

Christopher had followed me to the sandwich shop when I went for Bette's water. He got lost and began crying. A teenager took him to the lifeguard, but all the lifeguard could get out of him was that his name was Christopher and he was with "Mommy and Bette Davis."

In moments Bette appeared at the lifeguard's station. She was not alone. The entire beach had heard the bullhorn, and an entourage of autograph seekers followed her.

"Are you *the* Bette Davis?" the lifeguard said, rubbing a blob of sunscreen from his nose.

"I am the Bette Davis," Bette said. "Just as that young man on your lap said."

The lifeguard cleared a small area on the deck and for the next twenty minutes Bette signed autographs on damp napkins.

On the way home, Bette once again blasted Paul Newman for not extending the same courtesy to the fans who paid for his success.

"You know, Miss Davis," I said, as I summoned the courage to defend my favorite male actor, "Paul Newman has given millions of dollars to worthwhile charities from the profits on his salad dressing and spaghetti sauce."

"But Chef Boyardee will give *nnuh-thing* of himself!" she said, nervously clicking the car's metal ashtray.

"Rumor has it," I said, "that Paul Newman made it a rule never to sign autographs after he was followed into the men's room."

"And how many *thouuuusands* of times I've had to stop powdering my nose to accommodate a fan!"

"He wasn't exactly powdering his nose," I said.

"Mommy, was he doing pee-pee?" Christopher innocently asked from his car seat.

Bette roared with laughter. "Yes, young man," Bette said, "Paul Newman was doing 'pee-pee.' " Then in her exaggerated, choppy voice, she said: "Only small children can dethrone the high and mighty!"

The minute we stepped foot into our front door, Christopher darted to John's office. He gave him a blow-by-blow account of the afternoon.

Fortunately, Bette had just retired to her room for a rest when John came downstairs. He was carrying Christopher as if he were protecting him from a certifiable mother.

"Christopher," John said, "why don't you tell mommy what you just told daddy?"

"Bette Davis lost me at the beach!"

"Liz," John said, "would you like to elaborate on that?"

I told John the whole story. All the while I spoke, John kept looking at me as if I were one of those wacko women you see on the ten o'clock news, talking about how she left her kid locked in a Volkswagen with a German shepard for sixteen hours while she visited her boyfriend at a halfway house.

After an eternity of just staring at me, John asked: "What did you say to the woman who was supposed to be watching our child?"

"I told her exactly how I felt!"

"And?"

"I told her, 'All's well that ends well.' "

"That's really putting it to her, Liz!"

After all the afternoon's confusion at the beach it's a wonder I was able to get Bette to sit down quietly with us after dinner for the seance. That she was impatient is putting it mildly.

As I darkened the room, I could hear her snorting like a racehorse waiting for the gate to swing open at Belmont.

"Now we have to remember," I said, lighting

a candle, "that when you conjure up discarnate entities . . ."

"What the *hell* is she talking about?" Bette said to John, who was sitting at a rickety card table, leaning back on a small chair.

"Liz, explain some of the basics," John said with a marked rasp. "You can't just toss out buzzwords. You sound like a nut case."

Bette shifted her bulbous eyes toward John as if to say: I second that.

"Discarnate entities are people who have died," I said, ignoring John's superior attitude.

Bette remained mute. Her lips were pursed. Her hand was spinning her cigarette like a windmill. Her nervous gestures made me feel that at any moment she was going to storm away, and then I would lose ground in showing Bette the nonmaterial world.

"Okay," I said, "so when we talk to somebody who has died we should do so with the motive of helping them."

"Helping them?" Bette boomed. "Helping them *what*? Helping them float across Cloud Nine?"

"I know all this must sound really bizarre," I said, "but the theory is that spirit communication is a two-way street. For instance, we here on earth can bring comfort to those on the 'other side,' and those on the 'other side' can bring comfort to us."

"Kee-ryst, there she goes again with the 'other side,' " Bette said, inhaling enough nicotine to wipe out a brigade of laboratory mice.

"Unlike when we used the Ouija board," I explained, "we're going to have to all join hands because we're going to draw on our combined energies in order to contact someone who is no longer living."

"How quaint!" Bette said.

"But first," I said, "I'm going to lead you into an altered state of consciousness through a deep breathing process—"

"Jeeee-*sus*," Bette interrupted, "how long is *that* going to take?"

"Not long," I promised.

Just then the phone rang. It was my mother. She called to say that she bought Christopher a Cleveland Indians baseball jacket in size six so he could grow into it. She was taking Aunt Jean a two-pound box of Fanny Farmer chocolates to the nursing home. And Aunt Betty won twenty-five dollars at bingo. I cut my mother short, telling her that I was in the middle of bathing Christopher and I'd call her back. I certainly couldn't tell her that I was sitting in a seance circle with Bette Davis, especially since I hadn't told my parents that she was staying with us. I was sure that would be enough to prompt them to hop on the first flight out of Cleveland.

Before I could get my mother off the phone she gave me the third degree on who answered the phone last Sunday while John, Christopher, and I were at church. My father had phoned us, and Bette answered. My father asked to whom he was speaking. She told him in her thorny, crisp voice: "Bette Davis." Then she asked if there were any messages. "Yes," my father said, "just tell her Clark Gable called."

I told my mother that Bette's voice was just that of a friend who liked to joke around.

Back at the seance circle, I asked Bette if she had any questions before we began.

"What time is my hair appointment tomorrow?" she said, impatient.

"It's at eleven-thirty," I said, "with Mr. Bruce." Then I added: "I sort of meant, do you have any questions concerning the seance?"

"I am thoroughly *ex-haw-sted* from trudging the entire length of that Sahara desert this afternoon. My fingers are killing me. If I had to sign one more autograph they would have curled up and dropped off . . ."

Finally John came to my rescue.

"Bette," John said, "Liz is quite amazing in these seance circles. She never fails to get verifiable information that always checks out. And believe me, I'm a tough house!"

Thanks, darling, I said with only my eyes.

"Let's join hands now," I began.

"I just told you that my fingers are *killing* me!" Bette barked as she flicked a lit cigarette into the fireplace.

"Okay," I said, "no problem. We don't need to join hands." Then I spoke the usual sort of opening words for a seance. "We have gathered here with the highest purpose—to reach for and communicate with those we have loved in life . . ."

Once again Bette snorted like a racehorse.

"Let's begin by taking in five deep breaths," I continued. "Breathing in peace and love, and exhaling disharmony. As we breathe in peace, let's feel ourselves expelling all negative thoughts . . ."

I looked through squinted eyes for a moment to

see that Bette was not following my instruction. I continued the breathing routine anyway, trying to block out the fact that Bette was glaring at me as if I were one melon ball short of a fruit cup. Her pop eyes peering through the flickering candlelight gave me a bit of the creeps.

"Imagine," I continued, "that with each breath we are becoming lighter and lighter and going higher and higher toward a spiritual white light. Feel the group energy as we soar—"

Now Bette broke in. "The only thing that's missing is Shirley MacLaine," she muttered. "Jesus, if I see that woman on one more talk show drooling over her past lives I'm going to *vaaaahmit!*"

Finally I said softly: "If there is anyone who would like to come through, only for the good, we are open as channels."

Suddenly I felt the distinct presence of Bette's mother, Ruthie.

"Ruthie's here," I said with my eyes closed.

Bette made no comment.

"She's saying that death wasn't traumatic. 'I hung on to earth for quite a while. I didn't want to leave you . . .' "

"Kee-rist!" Bette said. "She held on too damn long!"

"Your mother is now saying, 'Bobby's here with me.' "

Bobby was Bette's sister, Barbara. In fact, Bette named B. D. after her. Although Bette had a love-hate relationship with both her mother and sister, she was magnificently generous in her support until their deaths. The moment Bette became a star with a star's bankroll, Bette showered Ruthie with furs, jewels, and a gracious house three times the size of her own.

"Ruthie wants you to know that she and Bobby are with you now," I said.

Bette seized on that one. "That's no surprise," she said. "They've got everything but Totalphone in the marble sarcophagus at Forest Lawn. It cost me a *bloody* fortune. I even have music piped in, for godsake!"

"This is a spirit far removed from Forest Lawn," I said. "They're actually living spiritual entities now."

"They sure as hell weren't spiritual when they were living off me!"

"Liz," John interrupted to say to me, "can you get anything concrete? Any verifiable names, dates, places?"

Once again I had John to thank for destroying the flow of communication with his journalistic hang-up.

"I'm afraid I've lost Ruthie," I said, furious with John. "She seems to be fading."

"That was *preee-cisely* why Harlow Morrell Davis left Ruthie!" Bette said in her most effective Bette Davis voice. "Ruthie was not Harlow's intellectual equal."

Bette's father was a Harvard Law School graduate who divorced Ruthie when Bette was seven and Bobby was five. Bette never forgave her coldhearted and aloof father for abandoning them, forcing Ruthie to support the family by working as everything from a maid to a photographer while Harlow made a hefty living as a patent attorney.

Bette also never forgave her father for not wanting her. In Bette's words, "Ruthie became pregnant on her honeymoon. Harlow was *enraged* that the hotel had no water for Ruthie to douche-me-away!"

My friend Robin had told me that she and Bobby once visited Harlow Davis at his Boston law office. Robin and Bobby, who were both twenty, made a special trip down from Maine just so Bobby could have a brief visit with her father, whom she rarely saw. Robin said that Bobby's father kept them waiting for hours. When he finally saw his daughter, he was cold, detached, spiritless, and short with her. They visited for only ten minutes. Robin said that all the while Bobby was growing up she craved her father's attention. Later in life Bobby would suffer repeated mental breakdowns. Robin felt that they were directly related to her father's lack of love. Bette, on the other hand, never sought her father's love and approval, at least openly. Unlike Bobby's fragile demeanor, Bette had an industrial-strength constitution that would suffer nobody. "You've got to have the *guts* to be hated," was her motto.

From the time Bette was a small girl, Ruthie had meticulously groomed her daughter to take on the world, and at all times beware that men were out to destroy her. Bette was a quick study in the evils of life and she picked up where Ruthie left off. Bette's credo for getting through life was: "You can sit by and let life happen—or you can *make* it happen. I'll take the latter, thank you."

The seance ended as downbeat as it began.

"So," Bette said, rising from the card table, "is that it?"

"If you're not too tired we could try to contact somebody else," I said.

"I think I'll try to contact Kathryn," Bette said, checking the time on her watch.

"Kathryn?" I asked. "Your secretary. But she's alive."

"Well if she weren't how the hell do you think I could contact her?"

I went to bed that night terribly disappointed that I blew a great chance at convincing Bette of a spiritual existence.

By morning, however, the spiritual world would also be light years away for me. Skipper's greeting to me in the kitchen punctuated this state of affairs.

"Mrs. Fuller," he said as he whipped a magazine from his back pocket, "it's a gosh darn shame what they're doin' to this lady."

It was a copy of *People* magazine. A full-color photo of Bette dominated the cover with a caption in king-sized type that blared: "Her daughter tells of boozing, brawling, and bizarre behavior."

"Get rid of that thing," I told Skipper. "If Miss Davis comes in here and sees that magazine all hell will break loose."

Skipper ignored me. He went on to say: "I was pickin' up a quart of milk for my daughter Claire when I seen this here magazine at the checkout counter. I damn near passed out. I says to the cashier, 'I was just fixin' the house where this lady's stayin' . . . '"

I interrupted Skipper to remind him that Bette could burst into the kitchen at any moment.

My warning had no effect on him. He flipped the

magazine open and read: "It says right here that she ripped a chicken apart. Threw it at her guests."

"Skipper," I hissed, "she's going to rip you apart if you don't get out of here with that magazine!"

Skipper, totally focused on the article, said: "Mrs. Fuller, have you read this scum?"

"Of course," I said. "I read it while standing in line at the checkout counter at the Food Emporium."

"You think Miss Davis has seen this?" he asked.

"I hope not," I said.

"I don't know why anybody would want to hurt such a fine, classy woman," he said, staring at her photo and shaking his head in disgust.

"Neither do I."

"She must be cryin' on the inside," Skipper said, wallowing in empathy.

At those words, Bette whipped open her bedroom door. In one move I snatched the magazine out of Skipper's hand and slid it into the silverware drawer. I intended to remove it later but forgot. When I remembered, it wasn't there. I assumed Skipper came back for it. But later in the day Bette said to me: "Darling, I've got your copy of *People* magazine. How appropriate that you placed it among your cutlery."

As she turned her head and walked back into her room, I noticed her shoulders sagging in a gesture that spoke loudly to me.

5

WORKING MAN

As the days turned into weeks, Bette slowly took over our lives. At least John claimed she did. In his pontifical words: "First, she arbitrarily decides the menu. Second, the time of the dinner. Third, whom we should invite for dinner, who should not be invited, and how Christopher should dress, behave, and the time for him to scoot into his toy room."

"Well, you've said yourself that our family needs structure."

"Structure is one thing," John said. "Slave driving is another. Every time I turn around you're chauffeuring her, running to Peter's Market just to bring her cookies, Carnation Instant Breakfast drink, and cartons of cigarettes. When you're not doing all that you're just staring at her with a vacant look of adoration—"

"I think you're jealous," I said to John, who was

buried in a stack of technical manuals for his book on tornadoes.

"Jealous?" John said. "I may be scared to death of her, but never jealous."

"I just wish you could see through her facade to the real Bette Davis," I said.

"We've been through this before, Liz," John said. "What you see is what you get."

"Bette colored with Christopher today," I announced. "You should have seen how sweet it was, John. Christopher went into her room with his coloring book and crayons, and said: 'Bette Davis, will you color with me?' I overheard Bette asking Christopher's advice on what color to crayon Mickey Mouse's ears. Cute?"

I didn't tell John that while she was coloring Mickey's ears she muttered to herself, "Christ, these ears have *nothing* on Gable."

I went on to tell John that they must have colored together for a full half hour. At one point Christopher said to Bette, "Bette Davis, you stay in the lines real good." Then finally Bette said: "Now young man, I think it's time you find your mother. If Bette Davis colors one more picture of Mickey Mouse my fingers shall curl up and drop off."

John was clearly not moved. "Get the Kleenex," he said.

"You just refuse to see her tender side."

"I refuse to see what's not there," John said.

"What do you mean by that?" I asked.

"Liz, you're fantasizing a relationship that doesn't exist—and will never exist. She desires a relationship with only *one* person: herself. And herself thrives on three things: high tension, conflict, and drama. Case closed."

I couldn't altogether dispute John's last statement. Bette had been in our house now for a full ten days, and the only time she really seemed to be enjoying herself was during some sort of crisis—like the time we lost Christopher at the beach. That minidrama awakened Bette's spirit of excitement and adventure. There was no doubt about it: Bette Davis was an adrenaline junkie.

I suddenly recalled how she had walked from the beach to the parking lot without using her cane. She was jaunty and chatty. She told me exactly how director Mankiewicz gave her the key clue to Margo Channing's character in one sentence: "Margo treats a mink as if it were a poncho." Then she clutched Christopher's hand as we searched for our car in the crowded parking lot under the broiling sun. "Mankiewicz," Bette added, "was always *furious* that he could never have *me* the way he had Crawford. *Evvverybody* had Crawford. It was a rite of passage. She was insatiable. Round heels!"

"Doesn't Robin have the mink coat you wore in *All About Eve*?" I asked, getting Bette off her favorite topic.

"That coat doesn't look *EN-Y-thing* like it did in the movie. After filming the studio gave it to me. I had the collar scaled down. About ten years ago I gave it to Robin."

"I *love* that coat," I said as I dragged the beach chairs, cooler, and sand toys through the parking lot.

"It was a marrrvelous coat!" Bette said.

Yes! I said to myself. For the first time she's *agreed* with me! I suddenly wondered if it was the adrenaline flow that put her in such a positive frame of mind, or maybe it was the fact that we were actually getting to be good friends?

Two days after our chaotic day at the beach, Bette's adrenaline was once again pumping full force. In retrospect, the whole chain of events that followed could have been avoided if Grover had only given us the message that John's grown son Judd had phoned earlier.

Judd had told Grover to tell us that he had a gig in Westport and would be staying over with us that night. Judd was a guitar player and singer in a country and western band. Although Judd had an apartment in New York City, he would often stay with us after a performance so that he wouldn't have the long drive back to New York late at night.

It was past midnight when Judd pulled his old Audi into our driveway. He took out his key and let himself in as quietly as possible so as to not wake us. Then he tiptoed into the guest room, not knowing Bette was sleeping there—something Grover failed to tell Judd.

When Judd got inside the room, he noticed that somebody was sleeping in the pullout sofa bed. Judd automatically assumed that it was his father. In the summer John would often sleep there, because it's much cooler than our converted attic bedroom. Judd didn't think twice about it, and he flopped on the sofa at the far corner of the room where he often slept. In minutes he was fast asleep.

Sometime around three o'clock in the morning we heard a bloodcurdling scream.

John jumped out of bed and called from the top of the stairs, "Bette, what happened? Are you okay?"

Immediately Judd's voice called out, "It's all right, Dad. It's only me."

"Judd, what are you doing here?" John said severely.

"Who the hell is Judd?" Bette roared.

"I'm John's son," Judd explained. "I'm really sorry. I thought Dad was sleeping in the bed."

"Judd!" John barked. "Why on earth didn't you let us know you were going to stay over?"

"I *did*!" Judd said defensively. He was wearing only a Jim Croce T-shirt and Fruit of the Looms. "I *told* Grover when I called in the afternoon," Judd added as he slid into his Levi's.

By now we were grouped at the bottom of the stairs. Judd was red with embarrassment. Bette was sheet white. She looked as horrifying as she did in *Hush Hush Sweet Charlotte* when she crushed her cousin to death with a giant concrete flowerpot. John looked as if twenty years had been skimmed off his life. And I was just plain petrified that this episode would be enough to make my idol pack her bags and call for her carriage convoy.

Finally John said, "Well we're just grateful you didn't call the police."

"I'm grateful I didn't have another goddam *stroke*!" Bette snarled, bugging her eyes toward Judd. "I woke up to the sounds of that man mumbling and snoring in my room."

Judd looked at Bette and went into a double take.

"You're not Bette Davis?" Judd said, shaking his head in disbelief.

"Well I'm not a madam running an all-night boardinghouse, for chrissake!"

Then I turned to Judd. "I just can't believe Grover forgot to give us the message that you were staying," I said.

Bette interrupted. "Your belief system is on shaky ground, my dear," she said. She was wearing a blue silk nightgown that had a large cigarette burn halfway down to the hem.

"I *told* Grover I was staying overnight," Judd cut in. "It's all his fault."

"There are few things that aren't," Bette hissed.

Once everyone calmed down, John and I went back upstairs to bed, Judd slept in John's office in a reclining chair, and Bette went back to her bed, grumbling: "This place is nothing but a goddam way station!"

The following morning when I came down to the kitchen to make Christopher French toast, I found Bette sitting at the breakfast table, energetically flipping through the *Daily News*.

"Good morning, Miss Davis," I said. I was sure that she was up early because her limo must be on its way. Quite the opposite was true, however.

"Well darling, it looks as if you're stuck with me for another day," Bette said with unbridled vigor. "Fish and guests both stink after three days, you know."

I looked Bette in the eye and said, "I was really afraid that after last night you'd want to leave this house of horrors."

"And I was thinking that maybe you would want to escape your chores for the day," Bette said with surprising good nature. "Ever since I've arrived you've been working your fingers to the *bone*."

"Not at all. I enjoy every minute of it," I lied, thinking that the moment we could stockpile some money, I would hire a maid, cook, and au pair.

"Is there any place special you'd like to go?" I asked. I could barely contain my excitement. For a split second I felt like asking Bette what she intended to wear—as if we were sorority sisters. But I thought better of that. There would be plenty of time later on for girl chitchat.

"I thought we'd just *explore* the Connecticut countryside," Bette said, taking a sip of Carnation breakfast drink. "As a Yankee I need an occasional transfusion from Hollywood glitz."

"What fun!" I said. "I'll get Samantha from next door to baby-sit."

Bette and I were in the midst of making our plans when Grover strolled through the front door, a plastic Dunkin' Donuts coffee mug in one hand and his toolbox in the other.

"Yo," Grover called, "anybody home?"

"Of course we're home, Grover," I said. "You see our cars in the driveway."

Hearing Grover's voice, Bette suddenly rose from the kitchen table. "Well, Mr. Mills," Bette said, throwing her shoulders back, planting her hands on her hips almost in a parody of herself, "your moth-holed memory turned this house into a Marx Brothers spectacle last night."

Grover looked blankly at Bette. Without saying a word he went over to the Mr. Coffee machine, lifted the carafe, and poured freshly brewed coffee into his mug. After taking a hearty swig, he said, "This coffee makes men out of boys." Then he turned to me and added, "What'd I do this time?"

"You forgot to give us the message that Judd called yesterday," I said sharply, nodding toward Bette.

"Did I forget to tell you that?" Grover said.

"You sure as hell did!" Bette exploded, "and furnished me with an unwanted night visitor as a result."

Grover chuckled to himself.

"Grover," I said, "in the future *please* give us all our messages."

"Well, if you expect answering service to be part of my job description, I'll have to hook it onto next month's bill." He chuckled again.

I could see by the way Bette bulged her famous eyes that she clearly did not appreciate Grover's flippant attitude. In an effort to patch things up between them I said, "You know, Miss Davis, you and Grover have something in common—you're both Yankees."

The word *Yankee* set Bette's eyes back into their sockets.

"Soooo Mr. Mills," Bette said, "I trust you'll live up to the tradition."

"I'm a real Connecticut Swamp Yankee," Grover boasted. "Fourth generation."

"And *I* a Lowell, Massachusetts, Yankee," Bette said, as smug as Grover.

I decided not to mention my dubious ancestry. In 1910 my Italian grandfather stepped off a banana boat with a hundred lire tucked inside his boot. And in 1917 my Irish grandfather sailed from County Cork on an empty potato boat.

"Lowell's not too far from Salem witch country," Grover said.

"Yes," Bette said. "Allegedly there was a witch in my family tree."

John poked his head into the kitchen just in time to hear Bette mention the witch in her family tree. As he poured himself a cup of coffee he whispered in my ear: "If she had been born two hundred years earlier she would have been burned at the stake."

"John," I said, dismissing his sarcasm, "did you know that Grover and Bette are both dyed-in-the-wool Yankees?"

"That's right." John nodded. "Bette, did you tell Grover about the old barn in New Hampshire you converted into a house?"

"It was a *beauty*!" Bette bragged. "All chestnut timbers."

"Some of the nicest homes I built were renovated barns," Grover said. Then he tapped an overhead beam and added, "This is a chestnut beam from a Connecticut Valley tobacco farm."

"And that's what gives this cottage *soooooo* much charm!" Bette said.

"A few years back I dismantled a barn in New Brunswick, Canada, that would have knocked your socks off," Grover told Bette. "I took it to Paris, Kentucky, and built an office for a horse farm."

"I *lovvvve* New England architecture," Bette said, pounding her fist on the table, accenting her point. "Those Yankee carpenters knew the beauty of functional simplicity!"

Suddenly Grover looked as if he had been pumped up a few sizes. He threw his shoulders back, straightened his Fairfield Lumber baseball cap, dug his thumb into his tool belt and said, "You guys oughta go poke around United House Wrecking in Stamford. They've got more bits and pieces of New England than a Yankee has money in his mattress."

"That's a great idea," I said. "I've been meaning to go there for years."

"Anything that gets torn down in New England, from a baronial mansion to a hut, ends up at United House Wrecking," Grover said. "They've got everything from barn doors and windows to trolley cars for sale. Last time I was there they had four authentic station master rolltop desks."

"It's settled!" Bette exclaimed. "Elizabeth, you and I shall get dressed and be on our way."

"Come to think of it," Grover said, "I've got to go down later on and pick up your front door."

"Maybe we can follow you down?" I asked, dreading the thought of aimlessly winding through Stamford looking for the place.

"You can do better than that," Grover said. "If you don't mind riding in a pickup truck, we can all go together."

"Grover," I said, "get serious."

"Hell, I've ridden in worse things than a pickup truck," Bette said with an intoxicating look of adventure in her eyes.

Shortly before noon Bette emerged from her room, dressed more for accepting an award than a trip to the junkyard. She was wearing meticulously creased white linen Valentino slacks, an Anne Klein II shirt, and navy pumps. The whole ensemble was topped off with pearl earrings and necklace to match. I suddenly hoped that Grover had the common sense to clean out the front seat of his truck. But he didn't.

"If you ladies just give me a minute I'll tidy up," Grover said, gathering up old McDonald's and Snickers wrappers, empty bags of Fritos, foam coffee cups, and a cluster of Yoo-Hoo cans.

"The inside of your truck looks like a recycling depot," I said, perturbed at Grover for keeping Bette waiting.

"For chrissake, he's a carpenter, not a chauffeur!" Bette said.

When Grover finally finished clearing out the front seat he said, "Okay, who wants to sit in the aisle and who wants the window seat?" Then he tossed a large plastic bag of trash into the back of the truck.

"Miss Davis," I said, "where do you want to sit?"

"Christ, just help me in."

"This is a bit of a climb," Grover said as he cupped his rough-hewn hand under Bette's delicate elbow and boosted her into the truck with a "heave-ho." Then I climbed in next to Bette, who was next to Grover.

"Watch your knees, Miss Davis," Grover said as he backed the truck out of the driveway. "This reverse gear shift is a real kneecapper."

"Jesus!" was her only comment.

As we headed down River Road, I felt like Sanford and Son going to the junkyard. At the stop sign at the end of our road, Bette reached into her alligator handbag and retrieved a cigarette. Grover eyed the "Thank you for not smoking" sticker on his visor and then reluctantly flipped open the ashtray, which was filled with screws and nails.

Approaching I-95, Grover leaned forward and turned on his CB radio. It was hissing and crackling.

"Why's that turned on?" I asked.

"Just want to hear the chatter," Grover said. "See where the Smokies are."

"Smokies?" Bette said, twirling her cigarette dangerously close to my face. The window was open, and I was suddenly afraid that the wind would blow the tip of her cigarette into my left eye, blinding me for life. But I would rather live out my life with one eye than say anything. I thought about how Sammy Davis, Jr. had lost one eye, and he had seemed to get around just fine.

" 'Smokies' is CB talk for cops," Grover said as if we should have known that.

Just then a large milk tanker trailer pulled up next to us. Grover immediately picked up the CB microphone and said, "How about it, milk truck? Do you have your ears on? Come on."

The response was instant: "I hear ya," said the milk truck. "Come on."

"I got you in my mirror," Grover said, adding, "Come on."

I couldn't tell if Bette was entertained or irritated by all of this. She did, however, widen her eyes and inhale deeply each time Grover and the truck driver said: "Come on."

"Do you have enough milk in that thing for a cup of coffee?" Grover asked. "Come on."

"I'm carryin' 6,000 gallons on my way to the Big Apple. Come on."

Finally the CB jargon got to Bette. "All right, what the hell does 'come on' mean?"

"That's CB talk for 'over,'" Grover explained. Then he said to the milk truck driver: "As soon as this stagecoach behind me passes you can pull back into the granny lane. Come on."

Bette was now sitting there like a smoking volcano getting ready to erupt.

"Who are the two seat covers with you?" asked the milk truck. "Come on."

"Mr. Mills," Bette said, erupting, "this is the first time I've ever been referred to as a 'seat cover.' I do not regard it as a compliment!"

"Same goes for me!" I said, as I gently nudged Bette's elbow.

"I didn't call you 'seat covers,'" Grover said, defending himself. "The milk truck driver did." Then Grover told the milk truck driver who we were: "Are you ready for this? I've got a friend, Liz Fuller, riding shotgun and Bette Davis jamming gears. Come on."

"Sure," the milk truck responded. "And I'm the Pope. Come on."

With that, Bette grabbed the microphone out of Grover's hand and said with proper venom and unmistakable Bette Davis inflection: "Fasten your seat belts, it's going to be a bumpy night! Come onnnn!"

"Hey that's pretty good," the truck driver said. "Who else can you do?"

Suddenly another truck driver cut in: "All right youse guys, how about this? Juday, Juday, Juday."

That capped it for Bette. "Turn that goddam thing off," she said. "It's giving me a splitting headache."

At the gates of United House Wrecking we were greeted by a scene that looked more like a Hollywood back lot than a junkyard. It was as if a time barrier had been crossed. Relics were scattered as far as we could see, including a complete subway car and trolley.

As Grover helped Bette out of the truck he scanned the horizon of the eight-acre junkyard and then said: "What-a-*dump*!"

"Give it a rest, Grover," I said, handing Bette her cane and handbag.

"Well, Grover," Bette said, suddenly calling him by his first name, "every dump should look like this." Then Bette tapped Grover on the arm with her cane and added, with a smile in her voice, "And be careful of stepping on my lines."

Walking through the enormous gate, I wondered if Bette would ever ask me to stop calling her Miss Davis. Sometimes I would concoct imaginary conversations between Bette and me where I would call her Bette and she would call me Lizzie. John called her Bette. I once asked John if he thought that I, too, should call her Bette? John just said that I should do whatever made me happy. He clearly wasn't putting any thought or energy into it.

"Hey, look at this horse-drawn cart," I said to Bette, who was eyeing a horse-drawn hearse.

"Maybe I should buy this hearse," Bette said. "They could hook this contraption up to a couple of draft horses and haul me off to Forest Lawn." She gave a roaring chuckle and then walked on to inspect an old trolley car.

"Here's an authentic trolley, all right," Grover said, giving it the Yankee once-over. "It looks just like the photos of the one my grandfather, Homer Mills, used to drive in Westport at the turn of the century."

Then Grover leaped inside the trolley for a quick look around. "My grandfather always told the story about how one day some kids tied a rope around the bumper of his trolley car and then attached it to the corner of the fruit stand. When my grandfather pulled away the fruit stand followed," Grover said, laughing.

"How quaint," Bette said in her indelible voice, not at all moved by the slapstick scene.

"Maybe we should go look for my front door now," I said, ensuring that Grover didn't continue to reminisce.

"Good idea," Bette said. "We shall look for just the perfect door for your enchanted cottage."

"All the doors and windows are in that barn over there," Grover said, pointing across the lot.

On first glance, I felt as if I had stumbled into a demolished church with all the stained glass windows, carved doors, and church pews scattered about.

After about twenty minutes or so, I said, "Okay, I give up. There's too much to choose from. You two decide on the door."

That was a big mistake. In retrospect I should have said, "Listen you guys, it's *my* door. I'm paying for it. Therefore I'm picking it."

"I found the door!" Bette called from the far corner of the barn. "It's a beauty!"

Within seconds Grover called from the opposite end of the barn. "I've got a door over here!"

"Elizabeth," Bette yelled, "come and look at your new front door."

Grover went over to inspect the door Bette found.

"This is a fine old door," Bette said with intense pride.

"Miss Davis," Grover said, "this door isn't even old enough to vote."

Bette took a half step back and snarled: "It's clearly all handmade."

"The only hands that touched this were the hands that took it off the roller after some machine spit it out," Grover said with amusement.

"How about all these fine molding details?" Bette argued.

"All machine made," said Grover.

"Mr. Mills, the panels on this door are definitely hand done!"

"No," Grover said, still condescending, "they were cut by a shaper, not a hand plane."

Bette was building up steam. "Well for chrissake what does your door look like?"

"Well as long as you asked," Grover said, "the stiles and rails were mortised and tenoned with wooden pegs as fasteners. Unlike your door, the panels were hand planed showing a beaded reveal on one side and a tapered backside to fit into a hand-planed dado in the stiles and rails."

"Look at the worm holes in this door," Bette said, cracking her cane against the panels.

"Those aren't worm holes," Grover said, lording it over Bette. "Those 'worm holes' were made with an ice pick. And those little squiggly lines were done with a bent nail and hammer."

Bette cut in: "Go get your damn door before you bore me to death!"

Bette was squashed in the debate and she wasn't happy about it.

After Grover paid for the door, I asked Bette if she would like to look around any further.

"I've had enough of a lesson in woodworking for one day," she snapped. "My feet were ready to go a half hour ago."

On the ride home, Grover and I both tried to entice Bette into a conversation. But she remained mute, other than to complain occasionally when Grover knocked her kneecap while shifting gears.

To exacerbate the situation, when we pulled into the driveway Grace's van was there waiting.

6

THE LETTER

"Well hallelujah, Praise the Lord, Grace is here, we won't be bored!" Grover said as he pulled in beside Grace's mission van.

"Leave the poetry to Skipper," I told Grover. Then I helped Bette step down from the truck. Once Bette was on solid ground, I told her: "I completely forgot that Grace was coming for an interview session with me."

Bette said nothing in return. She was still boiling over the door incident.

John came out to check the new front door. He looked on edge.

"This door's two hundred years old," Grover said proudly, holding up the door for John's inspection.

"And the life expectancy of a door is two-hundred-one years," John said. "How much is it setting me back?"

"About twice as much as a new door," Grover said, amused at John's cost consciousness.

"John," Bette said, "I heartily suggest that if you don't want to get involved in a half-hour dissertation on doors, you just drop it now." Then Bette turned to me and with piercing eye contact said, "You may tell your evangelist that I will be having a rest with the god of blissful sleep."

With those words, Bette made a beeline for her room.

Grace was waiting for me out on the back deck away from Bette's chilling glare. Sitting across from her under our Cinzano umbrella was Skipper. Grace was holding a pack of Camel cigarettes.

"When did you start smoking?" I said to Grace as we hugged hello.

"Well, praise God," Grace said with her usual enthusiasm, "Skipper just had his last cigarette."

"Is Skipper getting ready to go toes up?" Grover asked, putting on his tool belt.

"Skipper is going to ask the Lord to deliver him from his three-pack-a-day habit," Grace said. Grace looked and sounded as refreshing as a schoolgirl with her ever-present flower in her hair that matched the shade of her sundress.

"You should make it a two-for-one sale," Grover said. "Get Bette Davis off the smokes too. My truck, Beulah, could get lung cancer after today."

"Grover," Grace said, "why don't you and Liz sit down and we'll all pray?"

Grover bowed out from the prayer circle, saying that he had to place a lumber order. His Yankee skepticism did not allow for such celestial things.

Skipper, pleased with Grace's attention, asked, "Miss Grace, could we also pray that Miss Davis will give me an autographed picture of herself?"

While Grace prayed, my mind wandered from the scene with Judd in the middle of the night, to the junkyard scene, to another frantic episode that took place only three days before all that:

I had left Christopher at home with John while I went grocery shopping and to the dentist. John was in his office. I reminded him that Christopher was napping and to keep a close eye on him when he woke so that Chris didn't disturb Bette.

Not long after I left, John heard a rattling and rumbling in the kitchen. It was Bette. She was slamming cupboards open and shut as she made herself a midday snack. John, however, assumed that I had returned from the store and was putting the groceries away.

John was in a hurry to get to the library before it closed. He grabbed his car keys and called from the driveway: "I'm running to the library, honey!" Bette, thinking that John was talking to her, called back: "Okay!"

I returned home an hour later to find Christopher scampering around Bette's room, using her cane as a sword. One of her necklaces was draped around his neck like a chieftain's amulet.

"Where in Gawd's name have you been?" Bette asked between clenched teeth.

"The grocery store and the dentist," I said. I suddenly wondered why Christopher was in Bette's room when John was supposed to be baby-sitting.

"Nobody informed me that *I* was to be the nanny!" Bette snapped.

"Why isn't John with Chris?" I asked.

"Why isn't Damon with Pythias?" she barked.

Then with her usual vituperative energy she recounted the following: "I had just hung up the phone with Italy when I heard an ear-splitting crash in the kitchen. Christopher had christened the floor with a jug of apple juice. I almost broke my goddam neck mopping it up. I asked him: 'Young man, where-are-your *parents*?' That triggered an avalanche of tears. Christ, I thought he was never going to stop crying. *Finally*, I quieted him down in front of the television when the electricity went out . . ."

"Oh no!" I said. "How'd that happen?"

Bette clammed up. I suddenly realized that I had violated an unwritten rule with her. Nobody could ever ask her a direct question!

Before I could think of a way to retract my question, she swirled out of the room with pride and petulance.

Moments later, Grover emerged from the attic with an impish grin. He took inordinate delight in relating what had happened. "About forty-five minutes before you got back," he crowed, "our in-house movie star called up to the attic where I was replacing some collar ties. She asked me if I knew where you were. I looked out the attic window to the driveway. I told her that both cars were gone so both of you must be away. 'Jee-sus!' she spit out, 'I *know* that! Where the hell are they?' "

I had never seen Grover so animated. Like Bette, he luxuriated in conflict, turmoil, and irritation.

These character traits must be programmed into their Yankee genes.

Grover went on: "She was yelling something about broken glass. I come down to find the kitchen floor looking like a shoot-out at the Dead Gulch Saloon. She threw John's old tweed jacket on the floor to mop up the mess—"

"That's John's favorite jacket!" I said.

Grover shrugged it off. He went on: "I called Skipper in to clean up. That got her nose all out of joint. Then when I was placing an order with Bridgeport Glass, a call came through for her. She was giving the poor guy on the receiving end what-for. I thought I was gonna have to tranquilize her with my Marlin Perkins dart gun."

"What was the call about?" I asked.

"Something about a 'shit series called "*Hotel*," ' " Grover said, rocking back on his tan work boots. He was shamelessly basking in the situation.

"But what about the electricity going off?" I asked.

"I tripped a circuit breaker with my power saw," he said. "I was stuck up on the ladder in the dark. I called to her and asked if she could get Skipper out back and have him flip the breaker back on."

"You didn't," I said, recalling how Bette reacted to Skipper's last love note. It read:

Dear Betty,
I pretend to build this house
for you to show my love for
you is true.
          Love, Skipper

I told Grover she didn't even bother to crumple it as she did the last one. She just left it on the floor and walked over it.

Grover chuckled. Then he went on to say: "But what really got her pants in a bunch was when Skipper burst out of her bathroom with the gurgle and roar of the toilet flushing in his wake."

I told Grover to please tell Skipper never to use her bathroom again.

Grover's reply was in full character: "The only answer to that is to get a porta-john. That'll set you back an extra fifty bucks—not counting my override."

The sound of Grace suddenly shouting, "Thank you, Jesus!" over Skipper's Camels suddenly brought me back to the present.

"Liz," Grace said as she crunched the Camels, "Skipper won't be needing these anymore."

"What about Bette's cigarette habit?" I asked, looking over toward her room. I was startled to see Bette peering through a parted curtain watching us. Her sliding glass door was open. She must have heard everything.

Now, a week later, while driving to Peter's Market for a carton of Vantage cigarettes, I had to smile thinking about how Bette had peered through the curtain and seen Grace praying for her to give up smoking. That same night, Bette said to me, "Have a cigarette, darling, then Grace can pray for both of us."

Bette was a hard woman to read. I had expected her to be furious about Grace praying for her.

Instead she seemed to just shrug it off, to be almost amused by the whole thing. I had also expected Bette never to speak to Grover after the famous debate over the antique door. But the very next day she and Grover were chatting away about a 250-year-old farmhouse nearby that he was renovating. In fact when Grover invited Bette to see it, she accepted without a second thought.

Maybe where I was going wrong in my bonding with Bette was that I was so intimidated by her that I wasn't saying much of anything. Therefore she wasn't saying much of anything back to me. John, on the other hand, had developed quite an aggressive attitude toward her. She seemed to enjoy his countering her every move, as if they were champion chess players going for a title. The only thing Bette and John agreed about was that Little Ronnie Reagan, as Bette called him, reached a career peak when he starred in *Bedtime for Bonzo*.

As I paid for the cigarettes, I vowed to become more assertive. I had recently read an article that said if you wanted to be liked and respected you must not hide under a bushel basket. You must expose who you really are. You cannot always be so concerned with what others think of you.

Pulling into the driveway, I reminded myself of another important point the article made: like attracts like. I interpreted this to mean that if Bette Davis was going to choose a friend, she would choose somebody like herself. A person with substance. Fiber.

"Miss Davis, I'm back," I called through the crack in her door. "I've got your cigarettes. And I picked

up your black linen slacks from the dry cleaner,"
I said, adding, "They got all the bubble gum and
apple juice stains off."

"Good," Bette said, coming out to inspect them. "I
shall wear them tonight with my red silk blouse."

"Tonight?" I asked.

"Yes, darling," she said. "I told John that I'm
treating the two of you to dinner at Cobb's Mill
Inn. One of my favorite restaurants. And it's right
around the corner."

The old me would have said, "Wow, I adore
Cobb's Mill Inn." But the old me was not at all
appealing to a woman who had seen and done it
all. So the "new" me snapped, "They've never won
any prizes for their food!"

The moment those words left my lips, I regretted
it. Bette flashed a look that could turn the Ayatollah
into a gummy bear.

"Of course," I quickly added, "they're under new
ownership now and I understand the food is great."

"Get a table by the waterfall," Bette said as she
ripped the plastic bag off her slacks.

"Miss Davis," I called from the phone, "they don't
have anything by the waterfall. But the maitre d' can
seat us in the main dining room."

"My dear," Bette said, disgusted, "there are two
golden words."

The two golden words—Bette Davis—got us a
table practically under the waterfall. The maitre
d' was so obsequious on hearing the two golden
words that even I wanted to "vaaahmit." I thought,
no wonder Bette and I hadn't gotten really chummy.
I was as sniveling as the maitre d'. I felt fortunate,

however, that at least I recognized my mistake and now I had a chance to start over.

As I hung up the kitchen phone, I could hear Grover shouting to Skipper, "Get that lumber tied down and let's head up to the old Jennings Homestead."

Bette walked out onto the deck, looked up toward Grover on the roof, and asked, "Is that the 250-year-old farmhouse you were going to show me?"

"That's it," Grover said, dropping from the roof onto the upper deck. "How 'bout a private tour?"

Although I had planned on getting right to my office for a few hours of writing before it was time to pick Christopher up at preschool and get ready for dinner at Cobb's Mill Inn, I could tell Bette really wanted to see the old house he was working on, and so I told Grover that we would follow him up to Redding and have a look around.

"Watch your step when you get there," Grover cautioned. "The place eats tourists."

"Do you want the one-dollar or three-dollar tour?" Skipper asked Bette when we arrived at the Redding farmhouse. Bette pretended not to hear him.

"This is a beauty," Bette said, admiring a beehive oven and the fireplace next to it. The fireplace was trimmed in wide pine paneling. Old soft red brick framed it. The opening was as tall as Bette.

"It's a Rumford fireplace," Grover told us. "It's the most efficient fireplace ever designed. Designed back in Ben Franklin's time by a Count Rumford. This design here has never been equaled."

I could tell by the way Bette looked at Grover that

she respected his Yankee knowledge and appreciation for what she called "functional simplicity."

"Grover," Bette said, "tell me about this beehive oven."

"It was probably used for baking bread," I interjected.

"Christ, I know *that*!" Bette said. "What's it built with?"

"All hand-cast red clay brick," Grover said, tapping it with his fist.

"Let's get on with the tour," Bette said the moment Skipper stood next to her.

"Here's the keeping room," Grover said. "Legend has it that if someone died in the middle of the winter when the ground was too frozen to plant him, they would keep the body in this room."

"We had a 'keeping room' in the house I was born in," Bette said. "But I *nevvver* heard that one before."

While Grover and Bette exchanged Yankee folklore, I strolled in and out of various rooms, anxious for them to wind up the tour so I could get back to my work.

But then suddenly and unexpectedly something happened as I walked from the hallway into what was called the "Great Room." My head began to pound. I felt disoriented, dizzy, faint. I made my way over to a bench and sat down. I felt as if I might throw up. I could hear Bette and Grover talking in the background, but it was as if they were light-years away. I closed my eyes. Then suddenly I realized what was happening to me. I was experiencing the presence in the house of someone who had died. There was a ghost in the "Great Room" where I was now sitting. And I felt it was a troubled one.

I quickly recalled a similar thing happening to me once before. Several years earlier I went to visit a couple who had rented an old farmhouse in Georgetown, Connecticut, about fifteen minutes from my house. Their names were Ellie and Charlie, and they had asked me to come over because of strange things that were happening. In the middle of the night they would be awakened by someone playing Charlie's piano when nobody else was around. Ellie claimed that on several occasions her artwork was vandalized, either splashed with paint or cut. On visiting their home, I sensed that a tragedy had taken place in the living room. I actually felt the presence of a restless spirit. And as I walked from room to room I had the uncomfortable feeling that another tragedy was about to happen. I couldn't pinpoint what it would be. However on leaving I felt compelled to ask the couple if they had smoke alarms. They said no. I suggested that they buy some. About two months later, John and I were driving down the main road that led to their home. Suddenly several fire trucks raced by us. I had a sick feeling in my stomach and I said to John: "Ellie and Charlie's house is on fire." John did not believe me. *I* didn't even really believe me. But as we got closer, we both could see that indeed it was Ellie and Charlie's house. While they were out, it burned to the ground. Later Ellie did some research and discovered that an actor had hanged himself from the upper beam in the living room forty years earlier.

Now, back at Grover's antique house in Redding, I sensed the same sort of unsettling ambiance. Unaware that Grover and Bette had just entered the room, I said aloud, "Whoever is out there, could you please come through and identify yourself?" My eyes were closed. I still felt faint. "I sense a troubled spirit here—"

"Oh Jesus!" Bette roared. "Here she goes again."

"Welcome to the Twilight Zone," Grover added.

I was so determined to make contact with the restless spirit in the room that I ignored Bette and Grover and their flippant remarks.

"I'm here to help you," I said to the air. "If you have a message could you please channel it through me?"

"*Gawd*," Bette groaned, "she belongs in California. Every other person out there is 'channeling.' *Christ*, I never heard that goddam word before Shirley MacLaine made the round of the talk shows."

"I feel nauseated," I said, opening my eyes to see Grover, Skipper, and Bette staring at me.

"Mrs. Fuller," Skipper said sheepishly, "I think there's a ghost in this room too."

"Oh Jesus!" Bette repeated.

"Grover," Skipper said, "remember that letter that fell through a crack in the floorboards and settled down in the horsehair plaster ceiling last week?"

"Oh yeah," Grover said, "that old letter that talks all about the crops. Where is it?"

"I've got it in the glove compartment of my truck,"

Skipper said, as he bolted out the door to get it.

"Miss Davis," I said, reminding myself that the "new" me was no longer afraid to expose how I really felt, "I know you don't believe in ghosts or anything like that, but believe me, there's a troubled spirit here right now."

"Christ," Bette said, cracking her cane on the wide floorboards, "it sure as hell isn't Crawford! She wouldn't have the good taste to be in a place like this."

Grover chuckled along with Bette.

In moments Skipper was back with a piece of parched and stained paper in his trembling hand. He passed the letter to Grover to read. It was dated April 30, 1790.

Dear Aunt Prudence:

The promise of Springtime is finally apparent with the greening of the pastures and the blooming of the apple blossoms. On Saturday the children and I harnessed up the old chestnut and went down to the Chapmans to collect fiddleheads for a special Sunday dinner treat.

Everyone misses Uncle Ethan very much. He had such an unfortunate and untimely death at sea. Little Samuel treasures the scrimshaw carving Uncle Ethan sent him from South America.

We keep you in our prayers and hope to visit when summer has settled in and the planting is completed.

God Bless you,
Sara

"My God," I blurted, "there's the evidence that what I felt was accurate. I was feeling the presence of Uncle Ethan!"

"Oh Jesus," Bette said for a third time.

"Must have been a sea captain," Skipper said. He was still visibly shaken.

"Exactly," I said, "and that's why I felt so nauseated. I was most likely picking up on his vibration when he was sick at sea."

"For chrissake," Bette said, "what are fiddleheads?"

"Fiddleheads are springtime ferns," Grover explained. "They come out of the ground looking like the head of a fiddle. Old Yankees used to eat them. I tried them once, but they didn't have much taste."

"Grover," I said, "I don't want to alarm you, but I just don't have a good feeling about you and Skipper working in this house."

"Uncle Ethan was fish food two hundred years ago," Grover said, chuckling. "I don't think he's likely to be a concern."

Skipper did not appear to be taking my words so lightly.

"Mrs. Fuller," Skipper said. He was uneasy. "When I was here alone yesterday, I thought I heard footsteps goin' up the stairs over yonder," he said, pointing to the main staircase. "I thought it was Grover or Harold or Norman. I called, 'Grover? Harold? Norman? Is that you?' When I didn't hear nobody say nothin', I went up to have a look around. But there was nobody there. Then I started thinkin' that I imagined I was hearin' footsteps, and I grabbed my tools and started back to work."

The entire time Skipper told his story, Bette rolled her eyes and took exaggerated, impatient drags on her cigarette.

"I think I should perform a soul rescue to send the spirit's troubled soul onward and upward," I said. "I'm really afraid that Uncle Ethan is earthbound."

"Isn't that just ducky," Bette said.

"What's a soul rescue?" Skipper asked with a tremolo in his voice.

"A soul rescue is when you help someone make a transition from a physical reality to a spirit reality," I said. "The theory is that the spirit is still earthbound. The spiritual self still thinks it's in the physical reality. It hasn't faced the fact that it's a spirit."

"You're dead, Uncle Ethan," Grover quipped. "It's time to join the dirt people."

Ignoring Grover's wisecrack and Bette's incredulous stare, I went on to say that a sudden death out of normal time span could create a state of turmoil. The soul rescue was used most often by mediums in cases of a sudden or unexpected death.

"Brother," Bette said, losing patience, "stop talking about it and do your thing, and then let's get the hell out of here."

"The last time I did this sort of thing was in London," I said. "It was alleged to have been the most haunted house in all of England—"

Bette interrupted: *"Get on with it!"*

"Do I have to be part of this?" Skipper wanted to know.

"It's best if we're all part of it," I said firmly. "Our combined energies will boost Uncle Ethan's spirit into the spiritual realm."

"Call me when you've gotten rid of him," Bette said, as she and Grover exited to complete their tour.

Skipper sat down on the bench beside me. Then I led us into an altered state of consciousness through the deep breathing technique that we had used for the seance with Bette's mother. Skipper appeared so jittery, I was concerned that the deep breathing might make him pass out. At one point I could actually feel the bench shake.

"Skipper," I said, "do you want to continue?"

"Tomorrow I'll be workin' here all by myself," he said. "I sure don't want Uncle Ethan to keep me company."

"I don't think he's a malevolent spirit," I consoled Skipper. "Just a restless one."

With that settled, I continued with the soul rescue: "Uncle Ethan, you are no longer on the earth plane. You had a physical death aboard your ship over two hundred years ago. We have come today to help your spiritual growth. We are sending you up into the light—"

At that moment, Bette came into the room and announced flatly: "Your Uncle Ethan is on a door-jamb next to the beehive oven."

Hearing that, Skipper practically left his skin.

"What are you talking about?" I asked Bette.

"Miss Davis here just found Uncle Ethan's name

carved into the doorjamb," Grover said, as if she had just unearthed a buried treasure.

Sure enough, carved into a heavy chestnut beam was the name: Ethan Jennings. Next to his name were the dates, September 28, 1749–December 13, 1790.

"How on earth did you ever find that tiny carving?" I asked Bette.

"No doubt Shirley MacLaine and I lived here in a past life," she said as we headed out the front door toward our car.

7

THE MENACE

We arrived at Cobb's Mill Inn promptly at seven o'clock. One thing about Bette: she believed in being punctual for everything. "It's the mark of a pro," she said. Robin had told me that whenever Bette was invited out to dinner, whether to a restaurant or a private home, she arrived *exactly* on time.

"Christ," Bette said, ducking under the umbrella that John was holding, "this weather makes me wish I were in Cannes right now."

"Weren't you supposed to go to the Cannes Film Festival this year?" I asked, avoiding puddles.

Bette gave a sardonic laugh and said, "A public relations man tried to *persuaaade* me to go. He assured me of a standing ovation. I said to him, 'Darling, I can just walk across the *street* and get a standing ovation!'"

As we walked through the large barnwood doors at Cobb's Mill Inn, the tuxedo-clad maître d' and his staff of waiters were lined up in the entrance area at full attention, as if waiting to be reviewed by a general.

Bette nodded her elegant head. "Good evening, gentlemen," she said.

In unison the waiters bowed. No doubt the maître d' had rehearsed them.

"Please allow me to lead you to your table, Miss Davis," the maître d' said with a polished Latin accent. Then he added as if in an afterthought, "Mr. and Mrs. Fuller, please follow me."

I floated to our table, conscious of every whisper and every turn of head.

"Miss Davis, I do hope you enjoy this table," the maître d' said. "Our waterfall is on your left, the fireplace on your right."

"Quite nice," Bette said.

"It'll be fine," I added, matching Bette's tone of amiable indifference.

"Miss Davis," the maître d' said, "may I provide you with a brief history of our inn?"

"Shoot," Bette said, holding up her cigarette for a nearby waiter to dart over and light it.

"Cobb's Mill Inn is one of the oldest structures in the country," he began. "Its history predates the Revolutionary War of 1676. According—"

"*Sixteen* seventy-six?" Bette roared, then: "You'd better get your history books out, young man!"

"I'm very sorry," the maître d' said. He gathered his composure and continued, "The south end of the building was built between 1750 and 1775, and of course, the war was the very next year in 1776. But it wasn't until 1790 . . ."

Hearing the year 1790, Bette leaned over to me and jibed, "Isn't that about the time Uncle Ethan fell off his ship?"

"Who's Uncle Ethan?" John whispered.

"I'll tell you later," I said, turning my attention back to the maître d'.

" . . . The British Redcoats landed a thousand strong," the maître d' continued, unaware that he had lost Bette's attention. "They marched past Cobb's Mill in pursuit of the retreating forces of the Colonies, which fled—"

"How quaint!" Bette said, smashing her cigarette into the pewter ashtray. "*Where's* the menu? I-am-*staaarved*!"

"Yes, Miss Davis," the maître d' said, smacking the palm of his hand to call the waiter to bring us menus. "May I make a few suggestions about our house specials?"

"Please do," Bette said, taking a long and tolerant breath.

"For a hot appetizer, may I suggest Oysters Toscanini, a New England oyster topped with prosciutto, mushrooms, shallots, chives, our chef's own *secret* spices, and a Parmesan cheese sauce. Or perhaps, Miss Davis, you're in the mood for Clams Gruyere with fresh herbs in . . ."

The way he was addressing only "Miss Davis" made me feel as if John and I were the ghosts Marion and George in the the fifties TV show "Topper."

" . . . Our pheasant pate is a delicate . . ."

Bette cut him short. "You have Blue Point oysters?"

"Absolutely."

"I'll have those," Bette said.

"So will I," John said.

"I'll have the Oysters Tosca whatever," I said, asserting my individuality.

"May I say that those are very good choices," said the maître d'. "And now may I suggest a good wine?"

"Elizabeth, John," Bette said, "would you like me to order a bottle of wine?"

"None for me," John said. "I'll have an extra dry Beefeater martini. Sahara dry."

"And I'll just have a glass of dry white wine," I said.

"A wine spritzer for me," Bette said.

"With Perrier, of course?" the maître d' said.

"Christ, I don't care if it's Perrier or club soda!" Bette said, sending him on his way. "There's nothing I detest more than when a guest in my home asks for Perrier."

"If you want to be even snootier, you can ask for Badoit, also from France," John said, helping himself to a warm roll.

"Brother," Bette said, "I just got through saying I thought Perrier was an affectation. Why the hell would I want to ask for *Badoit*?"

"It's a better water," John bantered.

"According to *whom*?" Bette asked, prepared to fight this one to the bone.

"Any connoisseur would agree that Badoit is

superior," John said, groping. "I lived in France for six months and that's all I drank."

"There are people who have lived in America for eighty years and all they eat is hamburgers," Bette attacked. "Does that mean hamburgers are a delicacy?"

"Expensive champagne is highly overrated too," John said.

"*Any* champagne is overrated," Bette agreed.

I discovered that if I let John and Bette argue uninterrupted, eventually they would always come to a meeting of the minds. Both seemed to regard arguing as a creative activity—a game with its own aesthetic rules. I thought that until I could feel comfortable bantering with Bette the way John did, our relationship would never develop into a real friendship.

"Darling," I said to John, "you asked earlier who Uncle Ethan was."

"Yeah, who is he?"

"Spare John the unedited version," Bette said, speaking to the ceiling.

"Remember the old house in Redding that we went to today?" I said.

"The house Grover's renovating?" John asked.

"Yes," I said. "It's haunted." The old me wouldn't have been nearly as blunt.

"Is this where Uncle Ethan comes in?" John said, dipping a Blue Point into spicy tomato sauce. Then he winked at Bette and added, "Hope he's paying his room rent."

"Very amusing," I said. "Uncle Ethan was a sea captain who died back in 1790. But for some reason, he's earthbound—"

"Now Uncle Ethan is heavenbound!" Bette cut in. "He's on the *'other side'* haunting Crawford. She's had everything but a horny old sea captain!"

"Did she ever have Spencer Tracy?" I asked, just loud enough for the couple at the next table to stop talking.

"Christ, she almost *killled* the poor man!" Bette howled. "Everybody knew how aggressive she was in the sack. Their affair was kept no secret in Hollywood. Crawford saw to that. She got a perverse kick out of flaunting her conquests. I'll *nevvver* forget the night I walked past her dressing room, the door was open, and there they were. Crawford was all over him. *Killlling* him!"

"Did it last long?" I asked.

"How the hell do I know how long it lasted?" Bette blasted. "For godsakes, I only walked by the dressing room. I didn't hang there to see her going for the kill."

"No, I meant did their *affair* last long?" I said, glancing over at the couple next to us for their reaction. They were gaping.

"How the hell could *en-y-body* last with Crawford?" Bette asked, tearing the oyster away from its shell. "Tracy told *everybody* how she tried to steal his scenes every chance she got. But he got even with her. While she was in makeup for one of their 'romantic' scenes, Tracy slipped off to his dressing room and ate a raw onion." Then Bette downed the oyster and added, "Tracy was *always* quoted as saying that *I* was his favorite actress. That *buuuurned* Crawford's you-know-what."

I was just about to ask for an inside scoop on Tracy

and Hepburn when a family of four scrambled by our table. They were dead ringers for the family out of Chevy Chase's *Vacation II*.

"Here goes our dinner," Bette moaned, jerking her head toward the husband in lime green and yellow plaid slacks. Slung over his shoulder was a home video camera. His wife was at his heels in a skirt that matched his slacks. Two chunky children pushed ahead of the maître d' on the way to their table, which was less than ten feet from ours.

"Miss Davis," I said, "why don't you change seats with me so they can't see your face."

"Never mind," Bette smoldered.

The moment they were seated, the husband slipped a fresh cartridge into his video camera. Then he instructed his wife and children to stand by the window.

"I want Snookie and Harry Junior," he said, "to stand next to Mama and smile at those ducks. I'm going to zoom in for an extreme close-up . . ."

"Get a load of William Wyler," Bette said.

"I don't like ducks!" Harry Junior whined, as he munched on a roll.

"Get that piece of bread out of your mouth and smile at those ducks!" Papa scolded.

Just then the maître d' appeared at our table. "Excuse me, Miss Davis," he said softly. "I am very sorry for all this commotion across the way," he said, disdainfully looking toward the family. "They've had that table reserved for weeks. I would be happy, however, to move you to another table."

"I am fine right here," Bette said, dismissing his concern. "Is our dinner ready yet?" she asked, pressing her cigarette into the oyster sauce.

The maître d' smacked the palm of his hand once again and three waiters burst through the kitchen doors carrying our entrees.

"Miss Davis," the maître d' said as he supervised, "I do hope you enjoy your roast rack of lamb, and our secret rosemary sauce."

Bette mumbled under her breath, "Their 'secret' sauces make me feel as if I'm eating in the CIA commissary."

Once Bette's entree was meticulously placed before her, our dinners were attended to. My choice was the poached Norwegian salmon with hollandaise sauce. Nobody told me it was a "secret" sauce. And John had the roast prime rib.

Somewhere between my first and third bite of salmon, "Mama" at the other table sucked in her breath and said in a stage whisper: "Bette Davis is sitting right over there!"

"Mama-spotted-a-movie-star," Bette said in her most staccato tongue.

Harry Junior said to sister Snookie, "Mama says that old lady over there's a movie star."

For once Bette's eyes were narrow slits.

"How much film do you have left?" Mama asked Papa.

Papa checked his camera. "About half an hour," he said. "If I can reach an outlet, I can put the battery charger on."

"Jeee-sus!" Bette groaned.

"Who's the lady she's with?" Papa asked Mama.

"I can't see her face too well with all that frizzy

hair, but I don't think she's anybody."

My fifteen minutes of fame were up. I was back to feeling like the ghost Marion.

"What about the man?" Papa asked Mama.

"I think he's a producer," Mama said, sipping on a pink, frothy drink. She added, "He's all bald on top."

John visibly winced at that one. Then he gave a nervous cough and continued eating as if he never heard them.

"I bet that's his wife," Mama said.

Papa made some sort of comment to Mama but it was too soft to hear. I considered myself lucky. I couldn't believe that they didn't realize how their voices carried in the cavernous barn.

"Who cares about those stupid people!" Harry Junior cried. "I want a Coke."

"Shut up, *will* ya?" Papa said. "They can hear you."

"She's sooo skinny," Mama said.

"The camera puts ten pounds on people," Papa explained.

"Miss Davis," I said, embarrassed for her, "does this sort of thing happen wherever you go?"

"My dear," Bette said, taking a Vantage from a silver cigarette case, "I have had fans *faint* on merely seeing me in the flesh. Unfortunately that family over there is not the fainting type."

"It's not too late to move to a different table," I said.

"Papa has a zoom lens," Bette chortled. It was as if she suddenly saw the humor in the whole thing.

"There's a nice little dining room downstairs," John said. He was more ready to escape Mama and her comments than Bette.

"Now if I were Mr. Newman," Bette said, with the usual drag on her cigarette, "I would make a *Graaand* Exit. That way I would be assured of attracting the attention of every person in here tonight. You see, my darlings," Bette said, again spinning the cigarette, "Mr. Newman has a policy to *nevvver* sign autographs—so he must get his jollies in other ways!"

"Are you saying that if that obnoxious family came over and asked for your autograph you'd give it to them?"

"If they have the common courtesy to wait until I have finished my dinner," Bette said, setting strict house rules.

"It's such an infringement," I said, indignant.

"If I didn't like the side effects of stardom, I could have chosen to be a secretary. An *executive* secretary. I think I would have been quite good at that," Bette said, dead serious.

The more Bette revealed of herself, the more I admired her as a human being. I certainly could never have imagined Elizabeth Taylor entertaining the thought of being a secretary if she didn't make it in films.

"Bette," John said with a mischievous half smile, "you as a secretary is not something easily visualized."

"And what makes you say that?" Bette said, slipping on the boxing gloves.

"The first time you were sent for coffee, your boss

would end up in the burn unit at Mount Sinai."

"What you don't know about me is that I *adore* waiting on *strong* men," Bette said between clenched teeth. "It's the *milksops* of this world that I will not tolerate."

Bette thought of John as a strong man. The morning I drove her to her hair appointment she had commented, "Elizabeth, you're a lucky woman to have such a strong man." Feeling a little bit jealous of her admiration for John, I said, "He's terrific, but totally *useless* around the house." To which she responded, "Then why don't you just trade your John in on Skipper, and you'll have a handyman and a Cro-Magnon poet at your beck and call."

"Secretaries are grossly underpaid," Bette continued. "*All* the work and *none* of the glory!"

"Didn't you play a secretary in *The Man Who Came to Dinner*?" I asked.

"Over forty years ago!" Bette calculated on her fingers. "It was a wonderful film. With Monty Woolley."

"A classic," John agreed.

"Woolley was marvelous playing a delightfully wicked character," Bette reminisced. "He was a well-known radio personality who ends up by pure chance in the home of a typical Ohio family."

"That's where I'm from," I interjected. "Ohio. Cleveland Heights."

Bette ignored me, displaying her great capacity for being a selective listener.

"Woolley arrives with his secretary, Maggie Cutler," Bette said, adding, "That was *me*. He slips on some ice outside his host's home and he's carried inside shouting threats of a lawsuit," Bette said, giving a clipped laugh to the ceiling.

John, always ready to needle Bette, cut in to say: "Then Woolley goes on to amuse himself by re-arranging everyone's lifestyle." He pressed on my foot under the table, one of his not-very-cute ways to make sure I didn't miss the point.

"A good satire!" Bette said. Apparently she did not see the parallel.

"Miss Davis," the maître d' said, suddenly appearing at our table, "may I tell you about our desserts?"

Bette answered by widening her eyes and puckering up the red lips.

"Our chef has created special for this evening an Austrian chocolate soufflé," the maître d' said only to Bette. "We also have our *Soufflé au Grand Marnier* topped with the chef's very own secret—"

"My dear maître d'," Bette said, "by any chance is your chef's day job with the Secret Service?"

"No, Miss Davis," he replied, most seriously.

Bette retorted: "Before you wear yourself out hiding classified information, I'll have the chocolate soufflé."

"The Austrian chocolate soufflé it is," he said, practically clicking his heels.

"I'll have the same," I said, "but could you bring two spoons. My husband and I will share one."

"Absolutely," he said, disappearing.

I quickly turned to Bette and explained that I was watching my weight.

"And John," Bette inquired, "are you watching yours as well?"

"No," John said, tapping his gut. "I'm one hundred eighty-five. My fighting weight."

"So Elizabeth," Bette said, "you're going to pick at one soufflé like crows at a road kill?"

The old me would have been devastated by Bette's sarcasm. But the new me understood that Bette was merely trying to make conversation, and so I bantered right back in hopes of strengthening our relationship.

"The soufflé is better than eating crow," I said, wishing I had come up with a slicker line.

"Christ, if I hear those crows one more morning cawing on my deck, I'm going to curl up and die!" Bette said.

"They're better than the crickets," I countered.

"I adore the sound of crickets!" Bette said.

"I read somewhere that Nancy Reagan couldn't sleep because of the crickets," I said.

"If Mrs. Reagan can sleep with Little Ronnie I would think she could sleep with anything," Bette said.

"Including that mangy dog they're always dragging on and off helicopters," John quipped to Bette's undiminished laugh.

I was racking my brain to come up with a line to top John's crack, when all of a sudden I heard "Mama" across the room commanding her husband: "Zoom in as close to her face as you can."

I looked over to see "Papa" with his video camera resting on his right shoulder. The lens was pointed directly at our table.

"I just can't believe he's filming you without your permission," I told Bette.

"Why don't we have the maître d' tell him to knock it off," John said.

Without a word, Bette rose from her seat. She walked across the hardwood floor over to Papa. For several moments she just stood in front of him, glaring as only she could. Then she addressed him in her most effective, clipped speech: "Dear man, perhaps your zoom lens is inadequate for that distance?"

The family sat motionless. They were clearly more comfortable with Bette at another table.

"Are you ready to ask me to cross to the window and smile at the ducks?" Bette asked, throwing her shoulders back and positioning her hands on her hips in her twitchy style.

Finally "Papa" spoke: "If it's not too much trouble, the wife and I would like to get you on film with the ducks. Boy! I could show it to all my employees at my *chain* of paint stores."

He fumbled with his lens while his wife sat frozen. After the camera had rolled for only a few seconds, Bette abruptly announced: "Now I am going to return to my seat and have my dessert without the benefit of Candid Camera." With that, Bette walked back to our table in quiet dignity.

"You were great," I told Bette. In my next breath, I said, "I wonder what Paul Newman would have done if the same thing happened to him?"

Bette did not bite on my hook and line to draw her into disclosing anything more about Paul Newman. She simply raised her eyebrows as she picked up her spoon and sampled the chocolate soufflé.

As soon as John and I scraped our shared dessert

plate clean, I turned to Bette and said, "If you'll excuse me, I have to go to the powder room."

Bette nodded discreetly and went back to her soufflé.

On my way to the ladies room, I felt as if I were floating on a cloud again. My peripheral vision told me that I was the cynosure of all eyes. I suddenly wondered if maybe others thought my hair was overly frizzy too? I would have to talk to Anthony about a more relaxed curl for my next perm.

Standing in front of the mirror, I freshened up my lipstick, extending it just beyond the natural lip line to give my mouth that Bette Davis fullness. Then as I slipped my Lancôme lipstick back into my purse, I looked into the mirror to see Mama and daughter Snookie lurking behind me.

"Excuse me," Mama said, pushing her glasses up to the bridge of her nose with her forefinger. "Could my daughter and I trouble you for your autograph?"

"*My* autograph?" I said. I was completely stunned. "But I'm *nobody*."

"You're with *Bette Davis*," she said, passing me two unused envelopes that were embossed with miniature paint buckets.

Holding the envelopes, I suddenly wished that my grandmother was alive now to share the spotlight. I scribbled my name, thinking about how I used to accompany my grandmother to Mildred's Beauty Parlor every Saturday morning right after *Rin Tin Tin*. As Mildred finger-waved my grandmother's short gray hair, I would be in the chair next to her, leafing through a myriad of movie magazines, listening to Mildred and my grandmother exchange gossip about the stars.

When I handed the envelopes back to Mama and Snookie, they never even looked to see what my name was. I could have been somebody and they would never even have known it.

8

THE NANNY

When I got up the next morning, I was startled to find that Christopher was not in his bed. Moments later I found him in Bette's room. He was half under the covers, watching the Flintstones on TV. Bette was at her desk, writing the epilogue to her book that was mainly an answer to her daughter's book.

"I'm *really* sorry Chris has been bothering you," I said, lowering the blaring TV.

Bette looked up from a pad of yellow foolscap and said, "If I hear *Yabba-dabba-doo* one more time, I'm going to *vaaahmit!*"

"Let's go, Chris," I said. "You can watch TV in the living room."

"I'm staying here with Bette Davis!" Chris screeched. Then he squiggled down into the covers and popped his thumb into his mouth.

"You mean *Miss* Davis," I corrected.

"He means 'Bette Davis,'" Bette said, clearly enjoying the full-name reference.

For a split second I actually felt a bit jealous of my four-year-old son's relationship with Bette Davis.

"I'll give you to the count of three," I said to Christopher, yanking the blankets off him.

"Bette Davis promised I could stay and watch cartoons!" Christopher cried.

I began to count. "One . . ."

"For chrissake stop counting!" Bette sputtered.

"For chrissake mommy," little Christopher mimicked, "if you keep counting, I'm going to vomit!"

That stopped me dead in my tracks. I looked toward Bette for her reaction. She didn't appear to have one. Apparently she was immune to Bette Davis-ese.

"Christopher," I said, leaning over to pick him up, "Mommy is getting really angry."

Christopher squirmed away.

This time Bette got into the act. She went over to the TV set, flicked it off, and said: "Young man, 'Bette Davis' thinks it's time for you to go with your mother. Now *march*!"

Her economy of words and firm tone worked magic. Christopher leaped off the bed and scooted out, saving me the humiliation of dragging him out kicking and screaming—the usual scenario.

"You really have a way with kids," I said in genuine admiration.

"My dear," Bette said, "the worst mistake you can do is to *count*. *Evvvvverywhere* I go I hear parents counting, One-Two-Three! No wonder they never listen the first two times."

"You've got a point," I said, urging her on.

"Children do not feel secure unless you're *firm*," Bette said. "They need discipline if they're to survive in the world."

"I guess John and I have been a little lax in the discipline department," I admitted.

"Yes," Bette said with no uncertainty, "I believe you have."

"It just seems as if all those books on effective parenting are giving me mixed messages on discipline," I said.

"May I suggest you use your own good judgment," Bette said, complimenting me for the *very* first time.

"Did you have discipline when you were growing up?" I asked, trying to process Bette Davis's flattering remark.

"Ruthie was a *tyrant*!" Bette told me, quickly adding, "And so was I. It was a battle of the wills!"

I certainly didn't let on that Robin had already told me about how she and Ruthie went at it.

"Ruthie's life was hell!" Bette confided, returning to her desk. "She had Bobby and me and *noooooo* husband. I'll *nevvvver* forget the day Ruthie, Bobby, and I left on the train for Florida. I waved good-bye to my father from the train's window, not knowing that when we returned from our trip, Harlow Davis would no longer be living with us," Bette said in a resigned tone. Her eyes, however, seemed to reveal a piquant bitterness that I didn't expect from Bette Davis.

"It must have been just awful," I said.

"*Awwwwful!*" Bette said as she slipped on her heavy-framed glasses. "Ruthie moved us to over fifty apartments, furnished rooms, cottages, whatever. Gypsies!"

"But you surmounted all those obstacles," I said, suddenly aware that Bette's eyes were taking in the photograph on the back cover of B. D.'s book. It was a candid shot of B. D., holding her small son while Bette, the proud grandmother, looked on.

Bette slapped the book with the back of her hand and said: "*Whyyy* did my daughter do this to me?"

Her body language was so pained, I did not feel it was my place to comment.

"I loved that girl more than *annnything* in the world," Bette said, grabbing an unlit cigarette and swinging it like a lethal weapon.

"I'm so sorry," I blurted out.

My sympathy was clearly not in order.

She dunked the unlit cigarette into a cup of cold coffee and said in cast-iron Bette Davis: "What do *you* have to be sorry for?"

Suddenly I was in this deeper than planned. I told Bette that I was sorry because I could imagine the pain she must now be feeling.

"Well, young lady," Bette said, "don't exhaust yourself 'imagining' *my* pain!"

For fear of saying the wrong thing, I only nodded my head. Then I turned to leave. But before I reached the door, she called me back.

"Elizabeth," Bette said in an unexpectedly upbeat voice, "I'm in the process of writing the epilogue for my new book. It's an answer to B. D.'s epilogue. I want to read it to you," she said, picking up the yellow pad and clearing her throat. Then she began to read:

"I have much to quarrel about in your book. I choose to ignore most of it. But not the pathetic creature you claim I have been because of the fact that I didn't play Scarlett in *Gone With the Wind*. I could have, but turned it down. Mr. Selznick attempted to get permission from my boss, Jack Warner, to borrow Errol Flynn and Bette Davis to play Rhett Butler and Scarlett. I refused because I felt Errol was not good casting for Rhett. At that time only Clark Gable was right. Therefore, dear daughter, send me not back to Tara, rather send me back to Witch Way, our home on the beautiful coast of Maine where once lived a beautiful human being by the name of Barbara Davis."

"That's so moving," I said, choking back tears.

"You think I got the point across?" Bette asked with wide and pleased eyes.

"Miss Davis, you owe that answer to your *millions* of fans."

"I suppose you're right," Bette said. "I've received *hundreds* and *hundreds* of letters from devoted fans who are outraged—*outraged* by B. D.'s book."

"Boy, if my grandmother were alive today, you would have heard from her," I said.

"Your grandmother was a fan?" Bette asked, catching me totally off guard.

"The biggest," I said, thrilled that Bette Davis was finally interested in hearing about my beloved grandmother. "My grandmother is the one who first took me to see *Jezebel*. She saw *every* one of your old movies at least once."

"Is that so?" Bette asked, raising her pencil-thin eyebrows.

"Yep," I said. "My grandmother and I used to write you fan letters asking for your autograph. Then we used to trade those post cards your secretary sent, as if they were baseball cards."

I had Bette's attention and I was not about to stop now.

"I'll never forget the summer I graduated from high school," I continued. "It was the mid-sixties. Our family flew from Cleveland to California. It was our first plane trip. The second day I was there, I bought a road map of the homes of the stars—"

"Oh, those *miserable* bus tours," Bette gasped.

"Well I was crushed," I said. "Your name was not on the list—"

"Thank *Gawd*," she interjected.

"So I had to be content taking a tour of the movie studios."

"Those are quite nice," Bette said.

"Well, one of the studio guides said that she had actually seen Bette Davis come into the studio without makeup, and she was even able to get your autograph—"

Bette cut in: "Those young people work very hard."

"The guide told me that you wore three gold rings, but no diamond . . ."

"That sounds correct," Bette said, checking the authenticity of my story.

"That afternoon I took off my zircon ring." Bette gave a clipped laugh on hearing me tell her that. Then I went on: "Well, I was so excited on meeting someone who had actually met you that I phoned my grandmother back in Cleveland and shared the news. My normally soft-spoken grandmother let out a shriek that literally caused my uncle Bud to think someone had died."

"And how long has your grandmother been dead?" Bette asked, exhaling one large smoke ring.

"Fourteen years," I said. "We had a wonderful relationship when she was alive. But now it's quite different."

"*What* is quite different?" Bette asked.

"My relationship with my grandmother," I said.

"You just told me she's *dead*!" Bette barked. This time she moved her cigarette between her index finger and thumb, Groucho Marx style.

Here was my chance to explain the spiritual world to Bette. I felt the time was ripe.

"Anyway," I said, "it certainly appeared to everyone that she was dead—"

"Kee-ryst, is she *dead* or *alive*?" Bette asked irritably.

"In the physical sense she's dead," I explained. "But just because she's dead doesn't mean that she's no longer with me—"

"Oh Jesus," Bette said, rolling incredulous eyes to the sky. "I should have known better than to ask."

"Now before you start to pooh-pooh all of this, just hear me out," I said, reminding myself that

she'd respect me more if I spoke my mind, brusque-
ly. Then I continued, with all the passion of Shirley
MacLaine: "There's really no such thing as death.
It's only a transition into the spiritual plane. That's
the *true* reality," I said, avoiding those unrelenting
eyes. "I know you probably have trouble conceiv-
ing of this. I used to have great trouble picturing
a formless state with no physical body to support
a brain and mind—"

"*Ducky*," Bette quipped. "And *now* my 'physical'
body—or what's left of it—is *craaaving* a soft-boiled
egg."

I didn't want to delude myself, but I really felt
as if I had made some real progress. I would have
to be careful however, to not throw too much at
her at one time.

"I think I'll have an egg, too," I said, following
Jezebel to the kitchen.

"We'll use those egg cups," Bette said.

"I got those at a church tag sale for twenty-five
cents each."

"You already told me that!" Bette said, breathing
an exasperated sigh.

While I boiled eggs, fried bacon, toasted whole
wheat bread, and made fresh coffee, Bette meticulously set the table. She even plucked a handful of
impatiens from the garden for a centerpiece. Then
I called John and Christopher to the table. It was the
first sunny day in over a week, which put us all in
good spirits.

"Where'd you get the egg cups?" John asked as
he sat down next to Christopher, who was slouched
in his booster seat like Wolf Child.

"*Jeee-sus*," Bette groaned, slicing off the top of her eggshell. "If I have to hear any more discussion about those egg cups, I'm—"

" . . . going to vomit," Christopher completed her sentence.

"That's enough of that talk," I scolded. "Now sit up straight."

"I want Captain Crunch!" Christopher squealed.

"Mommy doesn't have Captain Crunch," I said, cutting up his toast and egg into bite-size pieces. "Now eat this."

"*No!*" he said, pushing his plate precariously close to the edge of the table.

"If he doesn't eat his breakfast," John said, "then tell him he doesn't go to Michael's birthday party this afternoon!"

That was one thing about John: all the discipline was filtered through me, as if I were the official bullhorn.

"Did you hear what your father said?" I asked, looking toward Bette for her reaction. She was on a slow boil. And as usual, her eyes told the whole story.

"I hate eggs!" Christopher said, ignoring my question.

"You like bacon, don't you?" I was fed up with his resistance.

"He can't get away with this every time we sit down to eat," John said.

At that moment, Christopher seized the butter knife and pointed it at each of us as if it were a semi-automatic assault rifle. Then he barked out his blood-bath jingle: "You're *dead*, you're *dead*, you're *dead*, I just pumped fifty bullets in your *head*. Here, there, everywhere, even in your underwear!" Simulated rifle sound effects and an eerie laugh followed.

Bette reacted with a look of genuine horror, feeding his burgeoning thirst for power. Just as he began an encore, I snatched him from his booster seat and swept him into his toy room. His dangling feet knocked the vase of fresh flowers onto Bette's lap.

"Elizabeth," Bette said, following us into the toy room, "*now* is the time to be *firm!*"

"Christopher," I said, my voice trembling with anger, "*I* feel very, very badly about what happened at the breakfast table."

"*You* feel very badly?" Bette roared. "*Brother*, I'm soaking wet!"

"Well, I never like to make any value judgment about his behavior," I explained. "The '*I*' message separates the deed from the doer. It prevents the child from feeling as if he were abysmally evil. '*You*' messages are always taboo."

"Your '*I*' messages are grooming the next gun-toting dictator!" Bette said as she soaked up the water on her white duck slacks with a kitchen towel.

Christopher heard the word *gun* and said, "I want a gun!"

"Guns hurt people," I said in futile protest.

"No, Mommy, they *kill* people!" A faint suggestion of delight was creeping into his voice.

"It's time for a '*You*' message," Bette commanded.

"Guns are bad," I said, trying to deal with reason.

"It's only bad if you *hit* them with the gun," Chris reasoned back. "But it's okay if you just shoot them! That's what Michael's mommy lets him do. So can I get a gun?"

"The *'You'* message!" Bette blasted. "Or you'll eventually be living under martial law."

"I can't do 'You' messages," I pleaded. "All my books warn that you're *never* supposed to criticize the child, only the deed."

"Young man," Bette said, taking over the discipline, "*you* have been *very*, *very* naughty. Such behavior will not be tolerated! And now, young man," Bette said, still firm but with a gentle edge, "Bette Davis is *staaarved*, so let us go finish our breakfast."

Christopher jumped up out of his bean bag chair as if on springs. Then he clutched Bette's hand, and together they went back to the kitchen, as tranquil as if they had just spent a day in the park.

"So what's on everyone's agenda for today?" John asked, enjoying Christopher's cooperative mood.

"Well, Christopher has that birthday party this afternoon," I said, "and I've got to go out shortly and buy the present at Child World."

"Maybe I'll come along for the ride," Bette chirped.

"Bette Davis," Christopher said, "Michael Gilbert is having a tae kwon do birthday party."

"And what is that, Master Fuller?" Bette inquired.

"You get to *kick* each other," Christopher explained with a glint in his eye.

"It's like karate," I said quickly. "The theme of the birthday party is martial arts."

"*What?*" John said, filling his cup with coffee.

"Michael's mother told me that she's having her son's tae kwon do instructor give all the kids a mini lesson."

"Liz," John said, "you know how we *both* feel about anything that promotes aggression toward another human being."

"Don't worry," I said, "it'll be well supervised."

John, a Quaker, didn't even allow a squirt gun in the house. I, however, was a little more relaxed about toy guns out of peer pressure. Virtually all of Christopher's friends had some sort of token arsenal in their toy rooms. In order for Christopher not to feel left out, I bought him a squirt gun to use only at the beach.

"There is something *sick* about a martial arts birthday party for a four-year-old!" John said.

"Christ," Bette said, buttering her toast, "if you wanted to see something sick you should have seen some of those birthday parties in Beverly Hills. Goddam elephant rides on manicured lawns! That's why *my* children were raised in New England."

"Michael told me that 'tae' means to kick and 'kwon' means to punch," Christopher said. His face lighted up with the prospect of going to the party.

"Liz," John said, "did you hear that? They're going to be kicking and punching each other all afternoon."

"Come on," I said, "lighten up. When I was a kid I never left the house without my Dale Evans holster and gun. In fact some of my happiest moments were spent going to the dime store for rolls of caps. To this day I can *still* conjure up the exhilarating aroma of burned caps. And I certainly didn't turn out to be a serial killer."

"Not yet anyway," John said, loading his pipe.

Christopher chimed: "I'm going to wear my tae kwon do jacket and belt to Michael's party!"

"Liz, you bought him a martial arts jacket and belt?" John asked, dropping his pipe to the table with a thud.

"He would have been the only one at the party without one," I said, nodding toward Bette. She appeared to be immensely enjoying the conflict.

"Great," John said, "we're in the throes of raising a thumb-sucking Rambo!"

"A Ronnie Reagan American!" Bette cackled as she left the kitchen.

As soon as I slid the breakfast dishes into the dishwasher, Bette, Christopher, and I headed to Child World to buy the present for Michael's party. Christopher insisted on wearing his tae kwon do jacket with its bright orange belt over white pajama bottoms.

"Well, Master Fuller," Bette said on seeing Christopher in his martial arts outfit, "you can be Bette Davis's bodyguard today!"

"What's a bodyguard, Bette Davis?" Christopher asked, climbing into his car seat.

"A bodyguard is a person who is hired to protect another person from becoming injured in a crowd," Bette told Christopher formally.

Whenever Christopher asked Bette *any* question she would always give him the textbook answer. She did not believe in talking down to children.

And she abhorred baby talk.

"I bet you've had your share of bodyguards," I said as we pulled out of the driveway.

"I was nearly mobbed to death *twice* in England," Bette said, rolling down the window and then lighting a cigarette.

"Were you mobbed by fans?" I asked.

"I wasn't mobbed by the Royal Mounted Guard for godsake!" A few moments later she said, "The English *adore* Bette Davis."

When we arrived in the parking lot, I asked Bette if she wanted to wait in the car. At first she said yes, but then Christopher persuaded her to come inside, saying that he wanted to show "Bette Davis" his most favorite store in the whole wide world.

"Well, if it's your most favorite store in the whole wide world, then you must show Bette Davis," she said, getting out of the car.

Christopher and Bette walked side by side. Bette was dressed all in navy blue—a marked contrast to Christopher in his all-white karate costume. He actually looked like her midget bodyguard.

As we walked through the entrance, I reminded Christopher of the rules: *no* G.I. Joe, and *no* weapons for Michael's present.

Like a bloodhound, Christopher made a beeline to the gun aisle.

"Look at all these cool guns," Christopher said to Bette. He was all but drooling.

"Let's go to the game aisle," I said softly so as not to draw any attention to Bette Davis. Practically every square foot of the aisle was taken up with kids frothing at the mouth.

Christopher, however, was not about to budge. He had found his bliss. "Read what the box says," Christopher said as he handed a carton to Bette. It was nearly as tall as he.

"*Brother!*" Bette exploded. "It's a five-piece realistic combat set, complete with an Uzi submachine gun, an M-16 rifle, a 9-mm Uzi machine pistol, and they've thrown in two hand grenades for the little monsters. Christ, it's recommended for five years and older."

A father in camouflage coveralls pointed to the box Bette was holding and said, "I got that for my youngest last Christmas, and the authentic firing sound on the Uzi machine gun was broke the next day."

He apparently did not recognize to whom he was talking. Bette bulged her eyes and responded in exaggerated Bette Davis: "Such-a-pity."

"Will you *pulleeeze* buy me those guns, Bette Davis?" Christopher asked, jumping up and down.

"Bette Davis does *not* buy guns!" Bette told him.

Suddenly a mother standing in front of a rack of sawed-off shotguns let out a death rattle: "*You're* Bette Davis!"

"Well, I'm not Duke Mantee with the Black Horse Vigilantes!" Bette said, referring to the 1936 film, *The Petrified Forest*, she starred in with Humphrey Bogart.

By now other parents and salespeople gathered around Bette in the gun aisle. Some were autograph hunters, others gawkers. Bette obliged her fans, but not without making a few snide comments about parents who buy their children guns.

It was late afternoon when I brought Christopher home from the birthday party. John was in his office talking to Bob Williamson, a close friend who was vice president of the Hyatt hotel chain. He was asking Bob, almost in a pleading voice, if he could get *any* inside information on a possible end to the hotel strike in New York. Bette was in her room having a rest after the hectic visit to the toy store. Her rest, however, was short-lived.

Christopher burst into Bette's room like a whirling dervish, performing a series of phantom side kicks accompanied by the tae kwon do battle cry, *keee-ya.* On one of his loose-legged side kicks he sent Bette's overflowing wastebasket into the air, spreading cigarette butts, ashes, cookie wrappers, and tissue smeared with lipstick across the rug.

"*Keee-ryst!*" Bette said in her own signature battle cry.

Before I could intercept Christopher, he jumped onto the bed next to Bette and with great delight showed her his party bag.

"Bette Davis, I got *two* packages of bubble gum!" Christopher said, spilling it out. "You can have a piece."

"Young man," Bette said, reaching for a cigarette, "Bette Davis does *not* chew bubble gum!"

Christopher said nothing other than to chew more loudly.

"Christopher," I ordered, "it's time you go to your room and calm down!" Then I turned to Bette and apologized. "I'm really sorry for all of this. I'll go get the vacuum cleaner, and then maybe you can get some rest before dinner."

"Not if that Cro-Magnon poet calls again."

"Skipper called?" I asked, surprised.

"He woke me from a sound sleep."

"What on earth did he want?"

"He kept me on the phone droning on and on about that goddam Uncle Ethan," Bette said, lighting a fresh cigarette from a still-burning butt.

"What did he say about Uncle Ethan?" I asked.

"How the hell do I know!" Bette retorted.

"I'll make sure he doesn't bother you again," I said, wondering what he told Bette about Uncle Ethan.

It wasn't until Monday morning when Grover arrived for work that I learned that Uncle Ethan had not been put to rest.

9

THE VIRGIN QUEEN

I was in my office when Grover strolled in, clutching his Dunkin' Donuts coffee mug and munching on a toaster waffle.

"Yo," he said, "I've got a problem."

"It can't be as pressing as mine," I said as I looked up from my typewriter. "You've got to install smoke alarms. Immediately."

I explained: "Bette set the living room drapery on fire last night. She twirled her cigarette into the edge of the hundred-percent cotton fabric. It was a miracle I was right there to plunge the burning drapery into her coffee cup before she was even aware of what had happened."

"I'll get Skipper on that," Grover said, appearing preoccupied with his own problem.

"So what's your problem?" I asked.

"Skipper's walked off the Jennings job," Grover

said as he tucked a pencil between his ear and baseball cap.

"Why?" I asked.

"He claimed that on Saturday morning, Uncle Ethan paid him a little visit," Grover said, rolling his eyeballs toward the North Star.

"Oh no!" I said. "That's what Skipper must have told Bette when he called late Saturday afternoon."

"He's telling everybody!" Grover said. "One of the biggest gossips in real estate called me this morning and wanted to know if it was safe to show the Jennings house."

"You're kidding."

"Two days ago a couple came back for the *third* time to look at that house. If they get wind of this, there goes the sale," Grover moaned, filling his mug with coffee from my thermos.

"I guess my soul-rescue didn't work," I said.

"Skipper's *very* suggestible," Grover said, dismissing the idea of a soul-rescue.

"Grover," I said, "as crazy as this sounds to you, I believe that Skipper was actually paid a visit by Uncle Ethan."

"Right," Grover said, "and I've brought in a crew of tooth fairies to rebuild your roof."

Ignoring Grover's remark, I went on to say, "The moment I set foot in that Great Room, I felt the presence of a very disturbed and earthbound soul."

"That's all Skipper has to hear."

"Don't worry," I said, "I'll talk to him."

"Whatever you do," Grover said, "don't get him any more spooked than he already is."

Just then Skipper pulled up in his truck. "I'll speak

to him now," I said, leaving my office.

"Remember," Grover warned, "he's *very* suggestible."

"Good morning, Skipper," I said, surprised to see Bette at the kitchen table reading the *Daily News*. She usually read it in her room. She didn't look up when I came into the kitchen, and she certainly didn't look up when Skipper slipped his lunch into the refrigerator and nodded, "Mornin', Miss Davis."

Before I had a chance to ask Skipper to come to my office so that I could talk to him in private, he blurted: "Mrs. Fuller, I'm still shaken up." He held out two gnarled, trembling hands to prove it.

Bette did not look up from the newspaper.

"Let's go in the other room and talk," I told Skipper, hoping to spare Bette the agony of hearing his story again. But Skipper was not about to move from the kitchen where he had Bette Davis as a captive audience.

Skipper began by saying, "Saturday morning I was up at the Jennings homestead. I was puttin' hinges on the doors. And when I passed through the Great Room I got a real cold chill zingin' up my spine. At first I couldn't see nothin' but I could smell the saltwater. As I was turnin' to leave I saw a mist beginnin' to form into the shape of a person. I never saw nothin' like it in my entire life. I started to shake so much I darn near thought I'd pass out . . ."

All the while Skipper spoke, Bette kept her head buried in the paper. Occasionally she would take a deep drag and make a short, loud puff into the paper. I could tell by the intensity of her puffs that she was building up pressure.

"Do you think this mist was Uncle Ethan?" I asked.

"Yes ma'am," Skipper said. "I could feel his bein' in the room with me as real as Miss Davis over there."

Bette looked so close to a major eruption that I was almost tempted to evacuate the house.

But Skipper went on, "I tore out the front door and ran smack into a real estate agent and a young couple goin' into the house. I says to them, 'You don't wanna be goin' in there now. That place has ghosts.' "

Hearing that, Grover erupted: "You told a real estate agent in *front* of a potential buyer that the house was haunted?" Then he slammed his tape measure down onto the kitchen counter. His face was beet red.

Suddenly Bette looked up from her paper. No longer was the morning dull and routine. Excitement filled the air. I could almost see the adrenaline coursing through her veins.

"Well, Mr. Mills," Bette said, "this is what happens when you hire poets instead of carpenters." Then she gave a cackling roar that not even the best Bette Davis impersonator could duplicate.

"So did they go in the house?" Grover wanted to know. Unlike Bette, Grover did not see any humor in the situation.

"I didn't hang around to find out," Skipper said, defensively.

"Mr. Mills," Bette said, with her endorphins fully activated, "your staff has apparently not read the do's and don'ts in real estate."

"Yeah," Grover said, "the closing costs will have to include a full-blown exorcism."

I asked Grover if that young couple Skipper referred to was the same couple who had already looked at the house three times.

Grover turned to Skipper and asked, "Did the couple's car have New York license plates?"

Skipper responded, "Yup—think so, anyway."

"Okay, that's it," Grover said, "it's the same couple. The deal is blown." Then he added, "Unless they're from Amityville."

Bette howled with the whinny of a high-strung stallion. "Grover," she said, "this fruit cake carpenter of yours is out of his wrapper."

Grover forced a chuckle and nodded his head in agreement. But I suddenly felt sorry for Skipper. Fortunately, however, Skipper was oblivious of Bette's acerbic tongue.

Before any more fun was poked at Skipper, I felt a moral obligation to come to his rescue, even if it was against my idol.

"Skipper," I said, not afraid to speak my mind, "I really understand how you must feel. When I helped John research *The Ghost of Flight 401*, I interviewed scores of pilots and flight attendants who claimed actually to have seen the apparition of the flight engineer who had been killed on Flight 401. And those crew members had really been shaken up too."

Skipper was listening so eagerly, I continued in spite of the fact that Grover and Bette were exchanging side glances.

"In fact," I said, "even an airline executive had an encounter with the dead flight engineer."

"Gadzooks!" Skipper exclaimed a millisecond after Bette groaned, "*Brother!*"

Undaunted, I went on to elaborate. "This executive boarded an L-1011, and found a flight engineer in one of the first-class seats. The engineer—or his apparition—looked up at the executive and said he was part of the crew of Flight 401. The startled V.I.P. went up to the cockpit to get the captain, and when they returned the apparition had disappeared." Then I added, "What do you guys think of that?"

"I think I may *vaahmit*!" Bette said, striking a kitchen match under Grover's oak table once again.

Grover piped up to say, "I think if Bette keeps scorching the belly of my oak table, *I* may *vaahmit*." He spoke with more affection than annoyance in his voice.

Bette gave a startled double take, not entirely amused. But then she leaned back against her chair and smiled to herself.

What startled me more than Grover's caustic comment was that he kept calling her "Bette." To all outward appearances it looked as if Bette and Grover were beginning to bond. And it was at my expense. It was Bette and Grover against Liz and Skipper. I thought to myself, what is wrong with this picture?

"Mrs. Fuller," Skipper said, digging into his coverall pocket, "this here's a pyramid I made out of copper wire."

"What's it for?" I asked.

"My lady friend," Skipper said with a quick, sheepish glance at Bette as if she might think he was cheating on her, "told me that this here pyramid would kick the tail off any evil spirits."

Bette darted a look that would wither any spirit in the room. Grover suddenly looked embarrassed that Skipper was on his payroll.

For some reason I felt obliged to ask Skipper what he intended to do with the pyramid. Later, however, I would regret it.

Skipper explained, "When Grover sends me back up to the Jennings Homestead, I'm goin' to press this here copper pyramid onto my forehead like this."

He showed us where he had put some sticky compound on one side of the pyramid so that it would stick to his forehead. Bette absolutely refused to look at Skipper with the pyramid stuck to his forehead.

Skipper continued, "I follow the Rapid Emergency Spirit Defense Procedure." He was reading from a torn piece of paper that his lady friend had given him. "I stand facing the direction of danger. I imagine my entire body cupped in a brilliant white light. I throw my arms out in front of me with the palms of my hands facing the danger," Skipper read. Then he demonstrated. He threw his arms out with palms directly at Bette. Bette, however, had her head turned as far as it would go. She was looking out the window and blowing smoke at the window panes.

Skipper looked so ridiculous with the pyramid plastered to his forehead, I could hardly believe Bette hadn't stomped out of the kitchen. Instead her face was distorted into an agonizing expression that could only say, "What the *hell* am I doing here?"

Skipper paused for a moment to study again the instructions on the torn piece of paper. Then he said, "I bring the tips of my two pointer fingers and the tips of my thumbs together to form me a pyramid, like this. Then I shout: 'I rebuke you in the name of Pyramid Power!' "

Grover winced. "Skipper's been working with asbestos for too many years," Grover quipped to Bette, who was seething and alarmingly silent.

"Skipper," I said with a touch of condescension, "I certainly hope that ritual will make you feel better." I turned to Bette and rolled my eyeballs, letting her know that I, too, thought this was nonsense. But my eyeball rolling was apparently too late. Bette's blistering stare told me that she had already lumped me into the same bag with Skipper.

Grover did not help matters any. He turned to Bette and said, "I suppose Janet from another planet here will want one of those pyramids too."

I snapped to attention and almost screamed at Grover, "I can live a full life without one!"

Skipper, not catching on to Grover's sarcasm, said to me, "Mrs. Fuller, I can make you a pyramid. No problem."

Grover jumped in and said, "Skipper's pyramid is about as effective as the meadow muffin he wore on his head to cure baldness."

"*Meadow muffin?*" I asked Grover. My eyes were fixed on Bette. She was gripped by one long, mammoth silent take.

"Yeah," Grover said. Then he turned to Skipper. "Why don't you tell them all about it?"

But Skipper was in no hurry to explain. Instead he grabbed his toolbox beside the refrigerator and left the kitchen, mumbling that he had to replace a rotted-out floorboard in our entrance hall. Grover, on the other hand, had no intention of letting the alleged cure for baldness remain a mystery.

Grover popped another waffle into the toaster and began to explain things: "When Skipper started to go bald he went to the doctor and the doctor, for a laugh, told him to wrap cow dung in a damp bandanna and wear it on his head for a week. A few days later his head began to itch and turn all red, and a few days after that layers of skin actually began to peel off his scalp—"

Bette cut in sharply at this point. "*Nevvver* before have I heard such nonsense! *Nevvver*. En-y-body who would stick a pyramid on his forehead to ward off evil spirits would slap cow shit on his head to cure baldness! I will not tolerate listening to such prattle," she said, getting up from the kitchen table and lobbing a lit cigarette into the sink stacked with dirty dishes. Then she stood directly in front of Grover, clamped her hands on her hips in her magnified, jerky style and said, "Mr. Mills, I have *seeerious* doubts about *you*."

Grover, towering a foot above Bette, suppressed a grin and retorted, "He's not a blood relative. And furthermore, Skipper and I don't use the same doctor."

Grover was clearly not intimidated by Jezebel. And Jezebel knew it. It was one Yankee against another. Bette gave Grover a token steely glare, and then she too suppressed a grin.

Once again, I was on the outside looking in. The problem was, I was not comfortable with confrontation. I had spent too many years in parochial school where submission had been drummed into every corpuscle of my being. Then I used to go home to a brother who ran a fascist dictatorship from his bunk bed. To further drain any possible assertiveness that may have lingered, I spent seven years in the airlines, giving toothy grins to every creep who said, "So where's the action tonight?"

As I continued to watch Grover and Bette come to a meeting of the minds, I could actually feel a tension headache begin to build. Consciously or unconsciously, Grover was horning in on my territory. Fortunately, John came into the kitchen just in time to throw a wedge between Bette and Grover.

"So is the time clock running?" John asked Grover, who was buttering his waffle.

Grover ignored John's question, saying, "How's the tornado book going, chief?"

"It's moving along quicker than the renovation around this place," John said with his pipe dangling from his mouth.

Grover reached into the refrigerator for syrup and said, "Do you want what you're paying for? Or do you want me to slop through the work?"

"Grover," John said, "how come I'm always on a deadline and you're not?"

Bette had been on her way out of the kitchen, but when she heard the tiff between Grover and John, her radar directed her to the center of turbulence.

"How can Grover possibly be on a deadline," Bette said, "when his chief of staff is at home making pyramids out of copper wire?"

I couldn't believe that once again Bette was referring to Grover by his first name. Regardless of the fact that she was now tearing into him, there was a bond developing between the two of them.

"Well, Miss Davis," I said, deserting Skipper's camp, "Skipper is a real nut case."

Hearing that, Bette did another one of her overwrought takes. But she said nothing. Grover, on the other hand, verbalized what Bette mimed, "Get a load of the pot calling the kettle black."

"Grover," I barked, "I may believe in many aspects of the paranormal, but I draw the line at 'Pyramid Power.'" Then I turned to Bette, smiled, and nodded my head in self-agreement.

Bette, however, was not in agreement. "There *is* something to the great Pyramids," she said with all the pontification of Carl Sagan. "When I made *Death on the Nile*, we filmed at the Pyramids. Christ, those things are impressive."

"There is definitely something to the pyramids," I said, doing a one-eighty.

"Brother," Bette spurted, "make up your goddam mind!"

"I believe in their power," I fumbled. "I'm just cautious."

"Cautious?" she said with eyes like heat-seeking missiles.

"I'm cautious about all this New Age stuff," I said, adding, "whether it's crystals, karma, or past lives."

Grover cut in: "I wonder what Bette was in her past life?" He chuckled.

"No doubt she was Queen of the Nile," John said, leaving the kitchen for his office.

"Yes, Mr. Fuller," Bette retorted. "And you would be the *first* one I'd behead," she said, giving an imperious glower that removed any doubt she would do just that.

"Miss Davis, I just loved you in *The Virgin Queen*," I said. "You were so convincing as the cruel Queen Elizabeth the First. And the makeup made you look bald."

"Look bald?" Bette flared. "Brother, they shaved my hair back two bloody inches to look like that hideous woman. But I've *nevvver* been afraid to take the nonglamour roles."

"I'm sure not many actors of your stature would feel that way," I said.

"Nonsense! Plenty of good actors would."

"Crawford wouldn't," I said, reaching for agreement on one point.

"*Jeee-sus*, don't start off the day with that name!" Bette said, ending all discussion of movies and actors. Then she peered out the window and said, "Today's the first hot day since I've arrived."

I only nodded my head, remembering that any discussion of the weather was taboo.

"To find out the weather around here you have to sit through ten thousand goddam years of Willard Scott's birthday greetings to toothless and mindless wonders," Bette complained.

"Hey, I've got an idea," I said. "Why don't we have a picnic lunch down by the river?"

"Now you're talking," Bette said, lifting my spirits higher than the Hollywood hills.

"I'll run to Peter's Market now and pick up fruit salad and a loaf of French bread."

"That's a smashing idea," Bette said. "And while you're there, I'll need a carton of Vantages. And *pulleeze* don't buy any more of those Pepperidge Farm cookies. If I eat one more of those I shall curl up and die."

Two weeks earlier she said the *exact* same thing about the Oreos.

"Keebler makes a real good oatmeal raisin cookie," I said. "And Famous Amos are excellent."

I was all set to tell her about Nabisco's double chocolate chip when those enormous deep blue eyes began to widen. Before she could squash me, I changed the subject from cookies to cheese.

"I'll pick up a nice Camembert, too," I said, grabbing the car keys and heading out the door.

At the river, Bette and I sat under our Cinzano umbrella on shaky beach chairs along the bank of the Saugatuck. The scene was reminiscent of a Cezanne painting, offset by a few duck droppings and mosquito nibbles. Wildflowers, bursting with color, covered the bank on the opposite side of the river. Occasionally a family of mallards floated by and shot over the waterfall, which was less than fifty feet from where we sat sipping dry white Chablis and spreading Camembert onto French bread. The only thing missing was Alistair Cooke to narrate the bucolic scene.

Bette was mellow. And for the first time I was

totally and utterly comfortable with her silence.

"You know, Miss Davis," I said as I took a deep, relaxing breath, "sometimes I have the craziest impulses."

Bette raised her eyebrows and seemed to shrug that one off.

I continued, "Like the other day while driving along the Post Road, I thought to myself: 'How long can I keep my eyes closed before I crash headlong into somebody?' But of course," I quickly added when Bette's head snapped toward me in one of her indelible double takes, "that sort of dark impulse is really quite normal."

I couldn't be sure if Bette's expression was one of horror. Or could she have suddenly realized that I was much more complex than she had given me credit for? I felt it was the latter, and I went on. "There are other crazy impulses I've had. For instance, sometimes I'm in the supermarket behind a doddering old lady and I think, 'Gee, I could just slam my cart full speed into her sacroiliac.' But as I just said, those impulses are terribly normal."

I helped myself to some fruit salad and said, "Here's something that's really sick: My sister has a pet bird and whenever he flies onto my lap, I think, 'Wow, how easy it would be to slowly squeeze the life out of him like a tube of toothpaste.' I sometimes will visualize his little tongue jutting forward in a death rattle. But then again," I told Bette, "we all have these thoughts, don't we?"

I was quite surprised when Bette made no comment. Instead she brought the palm of her hand up to her mouth and spat out a couple of watermelon seeds, grumbling, "How the hell can anyone eat fruit salad when it's swimming around in these miserable seeds!"

At first, I felt ridiculous for sharing all these dark thoughts with her. But then I thought: I will not allow myself to intellectualize about why Bette chose not to comment or share her own impulses with me. I was sure, however, that she must have recognized a kindred spirit.

I was reviewing all of this in my mind when suddenly a rubber raft skimmed down the river past us, carrying a man and a young boy.

"Now that looks like a good time!" Bette said, slicing off another chunk of Camembert.

"Well we could try it too," I said, as I pointed to our rubber raft that was a dinghy for our old sailboat.

Bette was noncommittal. She was much more interested in wiping off a speck of mud from her white slacks.

"Robin loves the river," I said. "She's always saying that this spot right here reminds her of Maine."

"Yes, it does," Bette said. "That's why I bought my house on Crooked Mile—downriver."

"How long ago did you live there?" I asked, although Robin had already told me.

"More than ten years ago," Bette said. "Michael met his wife while we were living on Crooked Mile. He would leave the house *early* in the morning and for the longest time I hadn't a clue where he was off to on foot. Then one day he told me that he had a young lady down the road. Chou-Chou is a *lovely* girl. She and Michael are very happy."

"If you want we could drive past your old house," I offered. "It's only ten 'minutes away."

"*No!*" Bette snapped, tossing her lit cigarette into the woods. I was glad it wasn't a hot, dry summer. "That place will only remind me of B. D. and my beautiful grandsons. Oh, the wonderful times we had at the river making mud pies. They *lovvvved* making mud pies." Bette dabbed the corner of her eye with a tissue. Then she regained full composure and said. "So *are* we going to have an exploratory tour in the wilds upstream?"

"Do you really want to?" I said.

"I just said I did!" she barked, rising from her seat at the picnic table and following me precariously to the rubber dinghy at the edge of the bank. "And for chrissake, keep your goddam eyes open!"

"Right," I said. "I only do that when I'm driving."

I was startled to notice how much air our rubber raft had leaked, but it seemed full enough to hold two lightweights for a quick turnaround on the water, which was shoulder deep at most.

10

WATCH ON THE RHINE

As I unhooked the raft from our large oak tree with roots half in the water, I suddenly felt a little bit woozy from the glass of wine. I wasn't used to drinking in the scorching sunlight or in the middle of the day, for that matter. It crossed my mind to postpone the boat ride, but I glanced over at Bette, and she looked eager for the adventure. I wondered if perhaps her two wine spritzers were now giving her false bravado.

"Miss Davis," I said, "Robin threatened that when she returns from Maine, she's going to borrow our raft and go fishing for trout. Each spring the state stocks the river with trout, you know?"

"I know that!" Bette said, shifting her weight.

"Maybe you'd better take off your shoes," I suggested. "All the rain we've had this season has made it awfully muddy getting in."

"So what?" Bette grumbled. "Now give me your hand and help me in for godsakes."

I held onto the bow with one hand and Bette's long, bony fingers in the other. Then I gingerly guided her down some firm stone steps—three, to be exact.

"Easy does it," I said, ready to catch her from plunging headfirst into the river. "You've got to be as sure-footed as a yak," I warned. "Robin got quite banged up on these rocks last year."

Although Robin and Bette were the same age, Robin jogged, played golf, practiced yoga, and swam in the frigid Maine water early in June. But then again, Robin had not had a stroke, a broken hip, or the mastectomy that Bette had had.

Gripping Bette's right hand and wrist, I thought of her indomitable spirit. In spite of her physical obstacles, she was willing to venture into a rubber raft. But it was quite a comfortable raft, with an inflatable seat and sturdy sides. Now as I took both of her hands to steady her before she stepped into the raft, I just wished that it had been inflated with a tad more air for a smoother ride.

"Where in the hell is the other oar?" Bette asked as she eagle-eyed the raft from the platform stone step that was our makeshift dock.

"We only use one oar," I said. "Because Christopher accidentally let the other one go over the dam, and it got away."

"Don't-take-me-anywhere-near-that-dreadful-dam!" Bette commanded. Then she cautiously lifted one rubber-soled shoe into the raft.

"Don't worry about that," I said. I used the left

side of my body to steady her right side as she got into the raft. "Even if we get real close to the dam, I can control the raft so that we'll be in no danger of going over."

"*Brother*, I hope so!" Bette said, perched on the inflatable midship seat.

I refrained from telling Bette that the tubby little raft had a tendency to spin like a pinwheel when I used only one oar.

"Now, Miss Davis, I'm going to pass you the oar. Then I'll get in."

Bette twisted her mouth, rolled her eyes, and grunted her okay.

As I was getting into the raft, I was surprised how much it sagged in the center with my weight, which was about twenty or so pounds heavier than Bette. Apparently my surprise showed.

"What's the matter?" Bette said, sensing my concern.

"Oh nothing," I said as I gave a wide, unnatural grin that undoubtedly annoyed her.

"Well let's get on with it, then," she said as she reached into her pants pocket for a cigarette and Bic lighter.

"Well! we're off!" I said, tossing the line on shore and taking the oar, which was resting against Bette's knees.

But we weren't off. The raft was caught on a rock bulging up through the rubber bottom.

"I'll just have to give us a little push off," I said, sliding over the side and into the water, which at this point was only knee-deep.

I gave it a firm push off the rock and into slightly

deeper water. "That'll take care of that," I said, climbing back in with dripping wet jeans and muddy feet.

Like a gondolier, I tried to push the boat upstream, leaning on the oar at the stern to prevent that awful spin. This, however, caused the bow to rise sharply in the air like a turtle peeking out of its shell. Bette seemed calm enough now that we were getting away from the dam.

"Every time I paddle upstream where the boughs of trees bend more thickly over the water, I like to picture myself as Katharine Hepburn and Humphrey Bogart on the *African Queen*," I said, adding, "What a film."

Bette answered with an explosive and derogatory, "Pffffff!"

"Well," I said, "it was a good film, but it wasn't a great film like *Jezebel*, *Dark Victory*, and *Of Human Bondage*."

"Bogart was a *vullllgar* excuse for a human being!" Bette snorted. She tempered her outrage by saying, "Hepburn is a lady! Gawd, how I envied that bone structure. What I wouldn't have done for those cheekbones."

"Me too," I said as I sucked in my cheeks to make my cheekbones more prominent. "But you know, there's no song out called: 'She's Got Those Katharine Hepburn Cheekbones.'"

Bette smirked in approval and said, "Darling, songwriters can twist en-y-thing into a song. Even I made an album."

"You did?" I said in surprised admiration.

"I'll have one sent to you," Bette said.

"I didn't know you could sing."

"Neither did I," she said with a pronounced drag on her cigarette.

I was just about to ask her what songs she sang on the album when my eye caught a large, dark glob inside the edge of the inflated side of the raft. At first I thought it was wet leaves lumped together. But on closer inspection it began to move. And when it crawled out from under the side of the raft, I was horrified to see that it was a huge, bulbous, gray-striped spider, about the size of an English walnut. I estimated that it was moving toward Bette's right foot at about the speed of an inch every fifteen seconds. My instinct was to let out a bloodcurdling scream and abandon ship and passenger. But my rational self—and more important, my airline training—prepared me on the way to proceed in an emergency: Never alarm the passengers. Speak in euphemisms. Take direct action in a way that will draw the least possible attention to the emergency. That would be a tough one now, I thought.

I did some quick figuring. If I could distract Bette for a very short time, I would be able to squash the spider with the flat end of my oar before she ever realized she was in any danger of being bitten by a possibly poisonous spider. I suddenly wondered if maybe it was a black widow? I thought I recalled reading in the local paper something about a little boy being bitten by one as he slept. But maybe it was a rat? I couldn't be sure.

"Gee, Miss Davis," I said, fighting off alarm in my voice, "if you turn your head just a bit, you'll be able to see the most beautiful purple and pink wildflowers on the opposite bank."

My strategy worked. "I had those same flowers on *my* riverbank at Crooked Mile," Bette said, observing the flora. But her interest was short-lived. She turned her head back in time to see me clumsily poking the oar inches from her foot.

"What the hell are you doing?" Bette asked.

I quickly recalled my airline training manual: "Receive complaints, suggestions, and criticism in a concerned manner and make all possible effort to relieve the situation. Passengers shall be given updated information to establish and maintain confidence in the flight crew."

"There's a nasty little bug I'm trying to help out of the boat," I said, careful to speak euphemistically but at the same time, provide my passenger with correct information.

She rolled those gargantuan eyes down at my fumbling attack with the oar. With a stroke of luck I was able to cover the giant, shiny spider with the flat end of the oar until she looked away.

Once again, I attempted to distract her. "Miss Davis, just off on your left is the cutest little island. Christopher and I call it Gilligan's Island."

I suddenly thought about that airline training manual again. It contained a full chapter called "Survival at Sea": "There is an abundance of food in the sea, and it is sometimes easier to live at sea than on small islands. Any fish you catch out of sight of land is good to eat raw. You can drink the blood, too. All birds are good to eat. Save their feathers to stuff inside your shirt for added warmth." For some reason I did not have a difficult time imagining Bette

Davis gutting a bird for its feathers—or guzzling its blood, for that matter.

"All you're doing is giving me a splitting head-ache, flopping that goddam oar around like a fish out of water," Bette said, lobbing a lit cigarette over my head.

"It must have scooted off," I said as I prepared to press the life out of it. But before I could do so, it squirted out from underneath the oar and took refuge back under the bulging inflated side.

"Damn!" I said, shoving my oar into the rubber crevice. "The little bugger got away."

"Brother!" Bette grumbled. "If you're so worried about a little bug you should have been on location in Egypt. I woke up one night to see the biggest spider I'd ever seen in my life."

"How big was it?" I gulped.

"The size of my fist," Bette said, squeezing her fist about a foot from my nose. Her pearl ring glistened in the sunlight.

"Are you allergic to spiders?" I asked, waiting anxiously for her reply.

"I didn't hang around to find out," Bette said. "The concierge had my room *fumigated* the next day."

"I wouldn't imagine that you'd be frightened by just a spider," I said, feeling her out.

"They-make-my-*bones*-shudder!" she said, ex-haling a plume of smoke.

"Spiders are really quite good," I said with a shaky voice. "They eat insects."

"So do bats, for godsakes! Does that make them house pets?"

As she spoke, I began to notice that the pneumatic sides of the boat were getting flabbier, like the skin of a wizened old man. I checked our position on the river, which was the worst it could be. With my oar out of water we were sliding downstream toward the dam. Fortunately, Bette's back was turned away from it so she didn't notice. It wasn't actually a huge dam—merely a three-foot drop, which was enough, however, to collapse the dinghy and leave Bette and me knee-deep in rushing white water with nothing to grab but sharp, slippery rocks. I didn't know if I should get the spider and chance the dam? Or get us away from the dam and chance the spider?

I would have to act fast. I gave the oar one final shove into the rubber crevice, hoping to squeeze this ugly little animal to death. Then I put the oar back into the water and poled us away from the drift. Thank God the raft didn't spin.

Less than a minute later the spider darted out, moving sideways and more bold than ever. This time it headed directly toward my bare foot. I cursed myself for not having worn my rubber thongs so that I could try to crush it.

While I was absorbed with this Indiana Jones escapade, Bette was giving me strict instructions on how to thoroughly towel dry the scallops for dinner.

"Yankees," she said, "are the only ones who know how to prepare seafood properly . . ."

I was nodding in agreement, but my eye was on the spider. It was only inches from my foot. My other eye was on the progress I was making against the current and away from the dam.

I gave a jerky kick on the bottom of the raft in a desperate effort to send the spider scurrying back to its roost. It froze in its tracks. Here was my chance for victory.

Bette, totally oblivious of the third passenger, asked, "Do you have flour and a spider?"

"A spider?" I asked, sure that she had spotted the stowaway.

"Yes," she said, short on patience, "a cast-iron skillet for the scallops."

This was no time to discuss gourmet cooking. Recklessly I pulled the oar out of the water, sloshing river grass and mud across Bette's knees and ankles. Fortunately, I just missed smacking her left shoulder with the blade of the oar.

Stunned by my unmotivated, convulsive actions, Bette threw her head back and popped her eyes to the size of Wiffle balls. "Elizabeth!" she said, no longer a happy little camper, "take me back to the shore at once!"

"I *got* it!" I yelled. I could actually feel the spider crunched flat.

Bette did not share my triumph. She sat mute and mad, looking down with disgust at an ugly biologic smear on the rubber surface. Then she commanded: "Get rid of that vile thing. It's the size of a small rat!"

"Yeah," I said, "it's like the rat you served Crawford in *Baby Jane*." I thought that if I could get her onto her archrival it would take the heat off me.

Bette lit a fresh cigarette from a half-smoked one, and lamented: "Unfortunately, I'll go to my *gravvvve* being remembered as the one directly responsible for insisting to Aldrich that he substitute a rat for a dead parakeet."

"But that was a great scene!" I said, attempting to lift the gelatinous mass with the oar before she could identify the body.

"I'll *nevvvver* forget the expression on Crawford's puss when she lifted the silver serving dish and saw the rat staring back at her," Bette said with a shriek of laughter that seemed to bring her immense pleasure.

"She must have nearly died," I said, quickly rinsing the oar blade in the river.

"Crawford was *never* informed of the switch," Bette reminisced with another wild shriek.

As I poled the boat toward shore, I said, "I can still see Crawford's eyes in that scene."

"Christ, how she overworked those dreadful eyes," Bette said, now overworking her own.

"But Kim Carnes never sang a song called 'She's Got Those Joan Crawford Eyes,' " I said, so obsequious I was ashamed of myself.

"Brother!" Bette said, "you just said that about Hepburn."

"No," I protested as I aimed the boat toward our "dock." "I said that about Hepburn's cheekbones, not her eyes."

"Whatever," Bette said just as the shrinking vessel came to a sudden, jolting stop.

"I'm afraid that the bottom has scraped on top of a little rock. But it's no problem at all," I said, careful not to alarm the passenger.

As I slipped over the side of the raft, my mind

flashed back to an airline emergency I had once encountered as a warning on how *not* to act: I had been working the first class cabin. The meal preparations had been spread out all over the galley. I even took over a couple of empty passenger seats to rest the makings for a salad. Sitting precariously above and near the 3-B seat were several cardboard containers of Thousand Island salad dressing. Without warning, we hit turbulence.

Everything went flying, including me. I was thrown against the forward galley, along with most of the meals. Before I had even a chance to check for multiple wounds, the man in 3-B began frantically ringing his call-button. I straightened up and glanced down at the front of my blue uniform. I looked like a Jackson Pollock painting. Dangling from my once-white ascot and down to my gold-buckled pumps were strands of lasagne. I stumbled over to my 3-B passenger, confused and dazed.

I couldn't believe what I saw. The man's eyes were glazed, and he was sputtering incoherently. Worse than that, there was some sort of yellowish gray stuff covering part of his scalp and dripping down the sides of his ears. It was the Thousand Island salad dressing. When we hit turbulence he got slammed with several cartons of it. But because of my confused state, I mistook the dressing for an open head wound, brains and all. On seeing the unfortunate businessman, I let out a primal scream that almost cost me my job.

Now, here I was, ten years later, but light-years beyond in maturity. "I'll have us on the shore in no time at all," I told Bette. Knee-deep in water,

I grabbed the bow of the boat and jerked it from the rock.

"Jeee-sus!" Bette said, jolted forward with the motion. "That goddam rock is poking me in the gluteus maximus."

"It's all smooth sailing from here on in," I said, maneuvering the flabby boat around several other slippery and slimy rocks.

"Hmmmph!" she said.

"We made it!" I said, pulling my irascible idol to the foot of our stone dock.

"Brother," Bette mumbled as she shakily stepped out of the raft and onto the rock that served as our dock, "a course in navigation and especially entomology is in order for you!"

"You know, Miss Davis," I said, realizing that nothing could escape those celebrated eyes, "when Christopher was eighteen months old, I was caught up in early infant development, and I bought him an ant farm to give him a broad sense of entomology. But he smashed the plastic case against the tray of his high chair and proceeded to lick up the tiny brown ants as they scurried off in all directions."

"Perhaps you should buy yourself a *spider* farm," Bette said, brushing mud from her Evan-Picone slacks.

Walking back to the house, I felt a few raindrops, but I said nothing about it.

"So I'll pick up the scallops for dinner," I said, "and maybe one of those good chocolate mousse cakes they have at the Lunch Box."

"This rainy weather is making me sick!" Bette said, flicking a raindrop from the tip of her nose.

I thought to myself: I refuse to be tricked into commenting on the weather. "Do we need lemons?" I asked.

"I'm getting drenched for chrissake!" Bette said, with gross exaggeration.

"I think I've got enough butter," I said, holding my ground.

"This is all I need, a cold," she said. "I'll be going to Italy with a miserable hacking cough."

Suddenly the sun burst through the clouds. "Look," I said, forgetting her admonition against weather talk, "the sun's out."

"I can see that!" she snapped. Then she checked her watch and said, "I have to call Paris."

I was glad John wasn't around to hear this. He had made it his unofficial duty to keep track of Bette's long distance calls.

While Bette went into her room to "reach out and touch someone" in Paris, I went to my office, compelled to write to my best friend, Sylvie Berkley. Sylvie was a Pan Am flight attendant temporarily based in London. Several evenings earlier, Sylvie had phoned me while she was on a New York layover. She was dying to know every little detail about Bette's visit. But I couldn't talk because I heard Bette breathing on the extension in her room—a chronic habit of hers.

"Dear Sylvie: [I wrote]
    Sorry I sounded so mysterious when you called the other day, but Bette was on the extension. I nearly died when you said, "I can't believe she's still there." But don't worry, she acted as if

nothing had ever been said. I guess she must feel a real need to eavesdrop because of the paranoia that goes with being famous. She probably thinks everybody is always talking about her—which they are.

The situation around here is getting progressively tense. John wants her out. He refers to her as "Satan's personal nightmare." He's a wreck that she's going to burn the house to the ground as we sleep and *she* smokes. Grover put in smoke alarms yesterday, but John's still grumbling. The day after she set the living room drapery on fire, I lent her my Irish fisherman sweater because she was cold, and she returned it with a huge gaping hole from her Vantage. God, do you know how much that sweater will be worth one day?

The good news is: Christopher and Bette are hitting it off. In fact before Bette arrived, Robin had told me that for some reason kids all adore Bette Davis. It's probably because of her voracious appetite for the outrageous. Christopher has even assimilated her clipped speech—along with a few of her more colorful expletives.

The other day when I picked him up from preschool, the teacher called me aside and said that during snack time one of the kids lobbed a paper cup of grape juice at Christopher to pay him back for knocking down his block tower. Christopher yelled: "Kee-ryst! Now-Christopher-Fuller-is-a-sticky-mess! I-think-I'm-going-to-*vomit*!"

When I came home and told John, he failed to see the humor. He said that nothing's less attractive than a four-year-old clone of Bette Davis. But on a more positive note, Bette doesn't let Christopher get away with a thing. She's the only one around here he listens to. I think that's what bugs John more than anything.

On the religious scene, Bette has let up on Grace. Now whenever Grace calls and says, "God bless you, Miss Davis," Bette will just toss it off saying, "Yes. Yes. Yes." I think she's taking all of her nervous energy out on poor Skipper, who really is making quite a nuisance out of himself. Yesterday morning he slipped another one of his "light verses" under her door.

Dear Betty:
You come here from movieland
and I hope you understand
I give you my hand to help
you when there is to much sawdust.
      Luv, Skipper

When Bette found it, she said in her best Jezebel style: "What-a-moron!" Then with her usual nervous stride and rotary hand movement, she added, "Send that toothless cretin back to the Black Mesa Bar B-Q."

She was referring to a seedy and dismal roadside service station restaurant in Oklahoma where she played the part of a waitress opposite Humphrey Bogart in the film *The Petrified Forest*. Sylvia, if you haven't seen that film, rent it. I've seen it six times!

She doesn't seem to have anything good to say

about Bogart. I don't know why she dislikes him so. I'm trying to find out. But I have to be casual about it. Whenever she senses that I'm digging for dirt, she clams up. She did, however, mention one evening after her third wine spritzer that Bogart was a lousy lay. But I couldn't tell if she was talking from experience or from gossip.

I really hope you can get a long New York layover and come up before she leaves. I don't know how much longer she'll be around. John's afraid that the hotel strike will last all summer. The first thing he does each morning is check the paper for news of the strike.

Well, I've got to run to the store for tonight's dinner. Bette's teaching me how to make a scallop dish—Yankee style. Her cooking leaves a *lot* to be desired.

I'll keep you posted on all further developments. I'm keeping copious notes. Love to Herb.

Love ya,
Liz

11

THE GREAT LIE

The following week went by without a major or minor catastrophe. I was sure that this sudden tranquillity would be a welcome respite for Bette. I was wrong. In the last few days she appeared to be terribly bored with John and me for our dull and routine marriage. John made a crack that maybe we should buy some breakaway dishes to throw at each other to spice up Bette's evenings—or her mornings, for that matter.

Now, as Bette and I were sitting at the breakfast table having boiled eggs and planning the evening's dinner, her negative propensities suddenly spurted into overdrive when John called down, "Liz, is there any coffee left?"

Bette looked up from her egg cup and gave me a shockingly blank stare. Then she said, "I suppose you're going to run upstairs to his office with coffee?"

"It's not worth an argument," I said to Bette as I reached for the pot, feeling the sting of her daggers as I did so.

As I poured John a fresh cup of coffee a black scene moved across my mind: *If* I dumped the entire pot of scalding coffee over John's head, could I possibly gain Bette's respect? Of course, I quickly dismissed that horrible thought when fantasy left and reality set in. The ambulance would arrive. Maybe even the police. There would be questions galore. My *only* reasoning was that I just wanted to win Bette Davis's deep approval and admiration.

When I went back downstairs to the kitchen, Bette flashed a look of contempt for my kowtowing to John's demand. I felt uneasy. To get her off my case, I said, "I was tempted to dump the whole pot of coffee over his goddam head!"

Semipleased with my aggressive attitude, she poured herself the remains of the coffee and boasted. "*All* my husbands beat me."

"Oh?" I said, very careful not to sound overly interested.

"Merrill and I used to fight tooth and nail!" she said as if she were talking about the good old days.

"Humph," I said, so offhand that she continued.

"One evening he *threeew* me out of the car. It was right into a twenty-foot snowdrift. I almost *died*! The drunken sonofabitch!"

Bette's words did not match her expression. Her eyes were literally twinkling with pleasure as she recalled that Currier and Ives evening.

"*Jee-sus*," she went on, "I had no boots on. No gloves. *Gawd*, that man could give a good fight!"

I knew that the minute I made any sort of comment, she would zip up those Bette Davis lips. So I said nothing.

"*Christ*, he was handsome!" she said, picking at a cinnamon bun.

"Mmmm," I said.

"Merrill fell in love with Margo Channing," Bette said, grabbing a kitchen match and striking it under the kitchen table as usual. She continued, "Merrill said that he walked around with an erection the *entiiire* time we shot *All About Eve*."

When she said that, I nearly choked on my English muffin. But nothing would stop her.

"Merrill married Margo Channing," Bette said, inhaling enough smoke to cause an ordinary mortal to pass out, "but he got stuck with Bette Davis!"

At this point, it suddenly occurred to me that perhaps I should share a slice of something steamy from my past as well. After all, I thought, if Bette was willing to confide in me, I should reciprocate to keep the friendship rolling.

"You know," I said, leaning forward but careful not to invade her air space, "when I was married to my first husband, I had a real passionate affair—"

Bette cut me off: "Shouldn't we be planning tonight's dinner?"

"Right," I said, feeling like a blubbering fool for actually thinking that Bette Davis would waste her time hearing about my sordid past.

"I thought that I'd broil chicken for dinner," I said, thumbing through an old, torn, and food-splattered Betty Crocker cookbook.

"If I eat any more chicken, I'm going to start to

cackle!" Bette said in her precise voice. "Don't you have *Joy of Cooking* for godsakes?"

"That's one book I'm afraid that I don't have," I apologized.

"Well that's *one* book you should have!"

"I'll pick one up tomorrow," I said, giving ninety percent and praying for a mere ten percent to be flung back at me.

"I shall buy it for you," Jezebel said, answering my fatuous prayer.

"Oh, that's very nice," I said, caught by surprise. If John were around to hear that he would no doubt mentally calculate how much Bette was costing us compared to the price of the cookbook.

"Tomorrow we'll lunch at Pierre's," Bette said, graciously giving one hundred percent to our relationship. "Then we'll stop by the Remarkable Bookstore for *Joy of Cooking.*"

"Terrific," I said, with just the right amount of indifference.

Once our plans were cemented, Bette dumped what was left of her coffee into the sink, rinsed her cup, and then asked, "Elizabeth, where can we get fresh raspberries for dessert?"

"It's the season for raspberries," I said.

"I know that!" she snapped. "*Where* do we get them?"

"I guess Peter's Market will have the freshest," I said. Suddenly, however, I recalled that my friend Gretchen had a huge raspberry patch at her country home in Ridgefield—only about twenty minutes away. Earlier in the week, Gretchen had invited me up to pick fresh raspberries. But I had been too busy to take her up on the offer.

When I told Bette this, her mouth watered and her eyes gleamed with the anticipation of sweet New England raspberries dotted in Devonshire cream.

"Well," she said, "what are we waiting for?"

Surprised, I asked, "You mean you want to come along and pick raspberries?"

"I have cabin fever!" she said, ready to rip the guts out of life.

Less than an hour later, Bette and I pulled into Gretchen's long driveway that led to her rambling Cape.

"Jeee-sus," Bette said, "this house looks *exactly* like the Cape I had in Bel Air."

"You had a Cape Cod house in Bel Air?" I asked.

"I called it Honeysuckle Hill," Bette said. "It sat among all those mausoleums, taj mahals, and stucco crematories with red tile roofs and twenty foot hedges sculpted into goddam bunny rabbits!"

Then Bette gave a lethal chuckle and went on to say, "I had my famous 'shit wall' in that house."

"Shit wall?"

Bette drew long and hard on her cigarette and then explained: "It was the wall where I hung photos of all those on my shit list. At the top of the wall going up the stairs was Crawford's mug. She had top billing. Then came Merrill's. Then Jack Warner—"

I cut in: "Did you ever run out of space?"

"Gawd yes! When that happened, I'd review the wall and decide who could be replaced." Bette continued, "Back in the midsixties the 'Today Show' came out and did a 'week with Bette Davis' at my home. The producer had asked me that very same question. I said to him: 'Mr. Morgan, could you please get me a photograph of Hugh Downs?' A few days later a large, autographed glossy of Mr. Downs arrived for my collection. I forget who he replaced," Bette said, dead serious.

"I bet Crawford never lost her space at the top of the wall," I said, shutting off the ignition.

I took Bette's silence to be a confirmation.

"Is your friend expecting us?" Bette asked as she stabbed her cigarette into the overflowing ashtray.

"Gretchen won't be home," I said. "But she gave us *full* permission to pick raspberries to our hearts' content."

Bette was very proper. She didn't approve of people who dropped in unexpected. But she seemed satisfied with my answer. "Well, let's get on with it," she said as she retrieved her cane from the floor of the front seat, and then waited for me to come around and open the car door for her.

When we got to the gate that led to the backyard, I found a note. It was from Gretchen: "Hi Liz, if you go in the house be *sure* to call the dog by name."

"That's a homey little touch," Bette snapped.

"Oh, we don't have to bother with the dog," I said. "We're not going into her house."

No sooner had I said those words than I began to rack my brain trying to remember the name of the dog. It was a Doberman with a German name. All I could think of was Heinz or maybe Franz? I knew it wasn't Hans. Hans was Gretchen's husband. He trained the dog to answer only German commands. Every time we went over he was yelling: "Plotz! Plotz!" And then, "Guten Hund. Guten Hund."

As we walked through the gate, I commented: "I guess the raspberry patch is in the backyard?"

Bette stopped dead in her Ferragamos. "You don't know where it is for godsakes?"

"Sure I do," I lied. "It's in the backyard."

I had a sudden fear that all the raspberries might have dried up. That fear, however, was allayed when we rounded the corner and came face to face with enough plump raspberries to make a Trappist monk break his vow of silence.

"*Keee-ryst!*" I exploded in my newly perfected Bette Davis. "Look at all those raspberries."

"*Keee-ryst!*" Bette said, surveying a raspberry patch the size of an Olympic swimming pool, "this is what I miss living in Tittyville!"

"These are the sweetest berries I've ever tasted," I said, sampling them alongside Jezebel. I expected her to tell me that they weren't as good as the ones in Maine. But she didn't.

"Quite tasty," Bette said, giving her Yankee approval. Then with great care she dropped them one by one into a number ten one-gallon tin can held by a string around her neck.

Before we left my house, Bette was adamant that we have the proper New England berry-picking equipment. I, too, wore a number ten around my neck.

"Careful of the prickles," I warned.

Bette snapped: "I've picked berries before you were born, for godsakes!"

"Did you ever make raspberry pie?" I asked, stepping into the brambles a bit to pluck the larger berries.

Bette separated the bush with her cane for me to get through and said, "There's a *marrrrvelous* recipe for raspberry pie in the *Joy of Cooking*."

"Great," I said. "I'll pick extras so we'll be able to make a pie."

"Splendid," Bette said, lighting a cigarette.

"We can buy one of those pie crusts already prepared," I said.

"Thank Gawd for modern miracles," she exclaimed.

With the late morning sun peeking in and out of the clouds, fragrant wildflowers scenting the country air, and Jezebel at my side blowing smoke rings, I could no longer deny the inescapable fact that deep down I was a clone of Bette Davis. With this startling revelation in a raspberry patch, I now realized why I had been so attracted to the character of Bette Davis. I had identified with her no-bullshit, tempestuous personality. She was the voice for my suppressed feelings.

Now with this sudden insight that Bette and I were not opposites but cut from the same cookie cutter, I could be honest with my emotions. For the first time in my life I could be *me*: a total bitch!

As I was trying to figure out how I could incorporate this new me into my spiritual beliefs, Bette let out a shriek to end all shrieks. She had sliced her index finger on the rim of the number ten tin can.

"Get me a goddam Band-Aid!" she commanded, as her finger oozed blood.

I quickly reached into my jean skirt pocket and slapped a tissue on the wound, then ran for the house as Bette called out sharply: "Make it snappy!"

I dashed through the kitchen door in search of the medicine cabinet. As I did the Doberman streaked by me with ears folded back as if they were stapled to his pointed head. In the emergency I grabbed a handful of paper towels and ran outside, frantically trying to recall the dog's German name.

The dog slid to an abrupt stop like a Road Runner cartoon the length of a forepaw from Bette. Bette lifted her cane and thrust it at the chest of the growling animal. Suddenly I remember the dog's name. It was Gunther. Then I remembered that Gretchen had once told me that Gunther would become enraged by the sight of a stick or a cane.

"Miss Davis," I yelled, "drop the *cane!*"

I ran toward the dog screaming the German command Gretchen's husband always gave: "*Plotz*, Gunther! *Plotz*, Gunther! *Plotz*, Gunther!"

This had no effect. Gunther began to slither on his hairless stomach toward Bette, making a guttural growl and baring his unfriendly teeth.

"*Get the fuck away from me!*" Bette yelled as she poked his chest just before she backed into a raspberry bush.

"You have to command him in German!" I told her.

"How the hell do I say *that* in German?" she asked in a throaty voice.

"Forget that and drop your *cane*," I ordered. "He hates canes! He was beat up as a puppy with a stick."

"Well now he's gonna get beat up as a grown-up," she said in desperation.

"You have got to drop your cane!" I pleaded to deaf ears.

I had half a moment to reflect: here was Bette Davis about to end her distinguished career as lunchmeat for some animal named Gunther. Unless, of course, I stepped in and took control.

"Get rid of that goddam cane NOW!" I commanded.

Bette seemed stunned. But the panic in my voice lent enough authority to cause her to fling her cane over the fence.

Miraculously, Gunther turned away from the defenseless Bette and ran toward the airborne cane, barking and growling at it as it landed in the driveway, about a foot from my car. Gunther didn't give us a second look as Bette and I cautiously backed away toward the gate to make a clean break.

Once we were safely in the car, I fully expected Bette to pulverize me to a fine dust. But again she proved unpredictable. All the way home she never brought up the incident. And I certainly didn't. Bette's only comment remotely connected to Gunther was that she would need to put an antiseptic and Band-Aid on her cut.

Back home, I went to our medicine chest to get the first aid kit while Bette went into the kitchen to drop off the two tin cans full of raspberries. John was at the table having lunch. As Bette cleaned her wound at the sink, she began to tell John about our adventure.

I was just coming into the kitchen when I overheard a quite distorted version of what had happened: "Elizabeth went into the house to do God knows what," Bette told John, unaware that I was around the corner listening. "The next thing I knew she released a mangy Doberman Pinscher. As the damn dog got near me, your wife started screaming his goddam German name: '*Plotzee! Plotzee! Plotzee!*' Then she started yapping for me to throw my cane to Plotzee so he could chew the hell out of it. She had that dog so worked up that he was frothing at the mouth and ready to kill us both. Your wife is a goddam hysteric! Thank *Gawd* I was there to get us the hell out of there in one piece. Besides all this the dog's name was Gunther, *not* Plotzee."

I could no longer tolerate listening to Bette's work of fiction. I swept into the kitchen. "Well here's some antiseptic cream and a Band-Aid," I said, feeling betrayed by my alleged friend.

I took a deep breath and blurted: "Miss Davis, there's something I feel *must* be cleared up—"

"*Brother*," Bette interjected, "what the hell kind of Band-Aid is this?"

"It's a Mickey Mouse Band-Aid," I snapped. "It's Christopher's."

Just as I was thinking How can anyone be so ungrateful? Bette went on to say: "How clever! Why didn't they have these charming Band-Aids when my kids were running to me crying over their scraped knees and elbows. My poor Margot was never without a scraped knee! How Margot loved Mickey Mouse."

Suddenly every bit of my resentment vanished. The mere mention of her retarded daughter, Margot, reminded me of the pain that must be pent up inside Bette. I thought about a comment she had made the day a handicapped schoolbus pulled up beside our car at a traffic light: "How can I pray to a God who has done *that* to those poor children?"

Now, after Bette wrapped her cut with the Band-Aid, she said, "Darling, what were you about to tell me?"

"I can't remember," I said, thinking that nothing could be gained by accusing Bette of her gross fabrication. Besides that, she was entitled to her opinion. Perhaps I did border on the hysterical? I was terribly sharp when I commanded: "Get rid of that goddam cane *now!*" In fact, now that I thought about it, I must have sounded like a real jerk screaming *Plotz! Plotz!* On the other hand, I did save her life. And maybe I should set the record straight?

"Oh," I said to Bette, "now I remember what it was I wanted to say."

"*Yes*," Bette said, pivoting toward me on the heels of her pumps. I could almost feel her eyes scorching the epidermal layer of my skin.

I took another deep breath and said, "I want you to know that I really admire the way you handled yourself in the face of Gunther."

"Knock off the admiration, sister, and get me a bowl for these raspberries!" Bette ordered.

The following morning Bette flung open the door that led from her room and announced for the entire world to hear: "Kee-ryst! that bed gave me the worst backache of my *life!*"

"Oh, hi Bette," John said, looking up from his bowl of corn flakes sprinkled with yesterday's fresh raspberries.

I jumped to immediate attention. "I'll have Grover

take a look at your bed the minute he arrives," I said as I stood by the stove scrambling eggs.

John consulted his watch and asked, "Isn't Grover supposed to be here by now?"

I still had not told John that three weeks earlier I had changed Grover's starting time so that Bette could have an extra hour of uninterrupted sleep each morning. I didn't think now was the time to tell him.

"Grover must be picking up supplies," I said. Just then I heard his truck pull into the driveway. "I guess he's here now."

"I hope he's had his breakfast," John groaned.

"Why should today be any different?" Bette said as she nibbled on a few raspberries.

Moments later, Grover appeared at the kitchen bar.

"Where'd you get the raspberries?" he asked, helping himself to a generous handful.

A red flag went up for Bette, who turned and glowered at Grover, making even him feel uneasy.

"As soon as Skipper gets here," Grover said, leaving the kitchen, "we're going to install those windows before it starts pouring rain."

With Grover out of sight, Bette appeared restless for some action. She began to pace like a Bengal tiger. She even looked like one.

"If it starts raining," Bette said, peering out the window, "I'm really going to vaahmit!"

John, ignoring the taboo against weather talk, said, "It sure looks like rain, all right."

"Of course it does!" Bette growled, whipping up some controversy to get the morning off on the right foot. "A moron can see that it's going to rain." Then she looked out the window again and came face to face with Skipper's truck pulling up. "In fact a moron is on his way into the house right now!"

"Mornin', Miss Davis," Skipper said in an obsequious, seductive tone.

"Hi Skipper," I said briskly so as to not encourage conversation.

"Boy, any minute it's goin' be comin' down cats and dogs," Skipper said, lingering in the doorway— only feet away from the object of his affection.

Predictably, Bette sucked in her breath.

"Grover's out back," I said. "He's been waiting for you to arrive with the windows."

"Holy moly!" Skipper spoke as Robin to Batman.

"You've got them, don't you?" I asked impatiently.

Instead of an answer, I got a story: "When I pulled into Fairfield Lumber this mornin', Stubby says to me, 'Skipper, Grover ain't ordered no sixteen over sixteens.' I says back to Stubby, 'Grover ordered them windows near three weeks back.' Stubby just started shakin' his head no. Then he gets on the horn to Shorty. Shorty says he don't know nothin' about no sixteen over sixteens. Shorty gets on the horn to the Big Boss. The Big Boss comes down from his office with all the order forms . . ."

I looked over at Bette. Her expression could have committed Skipper to life in a foam rubber lodge.

"Do you *have* the windows?" I pressed.

Keeping me in suspense, Skipper rambled on, "The Big Boss Man starts goin' through the orders. There was no order form for the sixteen over sixteen. Boss Man says, 'Skipper, I ain't got nothin' here.' I says to Boss Man, 'I was standin' right here the day Grover come in and give Stubby the order.' Boss Man calls Stubby down from stackin' lumber. 'Stubby,' Boss Man says, 'Grover Mills ordered them windows and I wanna know where in the friggin' blazes them things is?' Just then, Shorty comes runnin' over to Boss Man sayin', 'We got them sixteen over sixteens in the annex!' " Skipper finished, winking at Bette.

The intensity of Bette's glare bordered on the ghoulish.

John said under his breath, "That little yarn cost us twenty bucks' worth of his time."

"Well," I said to Skipper, "you'd better let Grover know you're here with the windows."

"Yup," Skipper said, giving Bette a longing once-over. "As soon as I put my lunch in the icebox."

"Jeee-sus!" Bette wailed, as she stabbed her cigarette into a decorative plastic Mother's Day plate Christopher had made at preschool. I could hear the plastic hiss as it burned. Then she snarled, "Elizabeth, we shall leave the house *promptly* at noon. Have you made reservations at Pierre's?"

"I'll do it right now," I said. Then I rolled my eyes toward Skipper as if he should be sedated and carted off.

As I picked up the phone, Skipper literally swaggered out of the kitchen, stopping only long enough to give Bette another one of his pining once-overs. This time it was accompanied by a double click out of the side of his mouth.

Bette looked so repulsed that for a fleeting moment I was glad she wasn't anywhere near the knife rack. She remained shockingly mute, staring savagely at her male caller.

To clear the air, I told Bette that I'd make sure Pierre gave us a quiet table out on the patio. Bette nodded her approval, but her eyes were still slinging poison darts at Skipper.

12

IT'S LOVE I'M AFTER

While Bette and I were lunching at Pierre's, Grover had promised to correct the sloping angle of Bette's pullout sofa bed before we returned.

"Well, Miss Davis," I said, taking a bite of my salmon, "tonight you're going to get a *good* night's rest."

Bette flicked away a few strands of hair from her forehead and said, "That miserable bed has given me a backache, headache, and nightmares!"

"Real nightmares?" I asked.

Bette sneered her reply.

Fumbling, I said, "I know that whenever I sleep on an uncomfortable bed, I have a *very* restless night. Lots of dreams. Some of them really weird," I added, thinking how stupid I must sound. In a frenzied effort to appear erudite, I said, "Freud says that an affect experienced in a dream is in *no* way inferior to one of equal intensity experienced in our waking life."

Unsparing of speech, Bette roared: "That man was a *lunatic!*"

"Yes," I agreed, "he erroneously attributed sex to absolutely everything!"

"On that score, I agree with him," Bette said, ripping off a hunk of French bread.

"Me too," I said, like a sniveling, gutless, spineless amoeba. I had about as much backbone as the salmon on my plate.

"Christ, I had a dream to end all dreams last night!" Bette said.

"Oh?"

"I dreamed Ruthie and I were boarding a train in Boston for Los Angeles. But once it started, the conductor came over and said in French that we were on our way to Paris. I gave him *hell!* I told him that the goddam train had *better* be going to California. I had to be there for a most important screen test. I stormed to the front of the train to speak to the engineer. When the engineer turned around, he was *Bogart* of all people! He said to me, 'We're going to *Paris*. You'll never make it in Hollywood, sister.' Suddenly I saw hundreds of American GI's surrounding the train and saluting. I demanded that the train be stopped. But we were over water. I marched back to tell Ruthie that we would be in Paris in a few hours. But Ruthie wasn't there. In her place was *Crawford*! Crawford was laughing maniacally while stuffing her bosom with Pullman towels . . ."

"That is *one* powerful dream!" I said.

"It's only a fucking dream!" Bette said, annoyed at my enthusiasm.

I summoned every ounce of courage and told Bette in grand academic tones: "Dreams are the activities of the unseen world of the *real* self."

"Dreams-are-a-pile-of-meaningless-*shit*!"   Bette said, biting her consonants in half.

"I know this is going to sound really crazy to you, Miss Davis," I began. "But about ten years ago my grandmother—not the one who was a big fan of yours, but my father's mother—had dreamed about a shoe box filled with silver dollars that my grandfather had collected over a lifetime. My grandmother said that my grandfather, who incidentally was dead, came to her in a dream and told her that he had hidden the box in our basement crawl space next to a 'piece of twisted metal.' "

I stopped my story long enough to take another bite of salmon. Then I went on in spite of Bette's gaping jaw and intense glare. "Of course nobody believed my poor grandmother—communicating with the dead and all. And certainly nobody in our family wanted to get on all fours and crawl into a three-foot-high space. Nobody except me, that is—"

Bette cut in to say, "*Why* am I not surprised?"

"Amazingly, just as my grandmother dreamed, I found a shoe box. It was coated with mildew and dust. It was also next to a broken fan, or as my grandfather told her in the dream, 'a piece of twisted metal.' Inside the shoe box were almost two hundred silver dollars, most more than a hundred years old. Later I had a coin from 1896 mounted onto a chain. I wear it for good luck. In fact I'll show it to you when we go back home," I said to Bette, who was staring at me with the blankest expression anyone could muster.

When the check came, Bette immediately plucked it up. Then she reached into her red clutch handbag for a personal check. After fumbling around for a few moments, she said: "Liz darling, I've stupidly left my checks back at the house. Would you be so kind as to pay this bill? I shall repay you when we get back home."

"No problem," I said, slapping down my American Express card on the red checkered tablecloth. As I did so, I slipped back in time. Suddenly I was no longer in Pierre's with Bette, but bumping along on a bus with my grandmother. We were on our way to the Cleveland Heights movie theater to see *Whatever Happened to Baby Jane?* We told my mother, however, that we were going to see a Doris Day movie. If we had been truthful, my mother would have checked the *Catholic Universe Bulletin*, and seen that *Whatever Happened to Baby Jane?* was disapproved for Catholics of any age. Our parish priest, who would have been great living in a police state, made his congregation pledge to follow the standards outlined in the C.U.B.—or they would fry in hell. My grandmother said that she would sooner fry in hell than sit through two hours of Doris Day.

For weeks before we actually saw Bette Davis in her first horror film, my grandmother would feed me the movie magazine gossip about how grotesque Bette Davis's makeup and costumes were, how Bette Davis and Joan Crawford carried on like certifiable loonies, and how one movie magazine suggested that if you had a bad heart—skip this movie.

After the bus had dropped us off, my grand-mother and I waited under the marquee until the box office opened. Then we swept into the theater, stopping at the candy counter for a large box of Milk Duds for me. My grandmother brown-bagged it with homemade popcorn.

By the time the house lights dimmed, my grand-mother and I were pressed shoulder to shoulder ready to be scared to death by the woman who drew us the way a magnet pulls iron filings.

Looking at Bette across the table, smearing on scarlet lipstick from a Lancôme tube, I could hardly believe the chain of events that brought my idol to me. Was our meeting predestined? And if it was, then what was the lesson I was supposed to be learning?

As I was mulling that one over, Bette blotted her lips with the cloth napkin and said, "*Damn*, we won't be able to pick up *Joy of Cooking* since I've forgotten my checks."

"Oh don't be silly," I said, "I'll buy it."

"You will not! We'll get it later in the week."

When Bette said, "later in the week," I thought of poor John and the emotional turmoil he was putting himself through trying to cope with our "recklessly outspoken" houseguest.

The previous night, as John and I were getting ready for bed, I became concerned about his col-oring.

"You look gray," I told him.

"I'm only reflecting the atmosphere," John said as he reached for the Maalox bottle.

John was doing everything in his power to end Bette's visit. His last ploy was to place several books on charming New England inns strategically wherever she might see them—on the coffee table, kitchen table, next to the phone. I was afraid he was going to place one on her pillow with a chocolate mint.

When Bette paid no attention to the books, John had the nerve to say, "Gee Bette, can you believe that right in our own backyard are some of the most gracious inns in the entire country? Cozy bed and breakfast inns—all with fireplaces . . ."

Fortunately, Bette wasn't tuned in to his rudeness. Her typical reply was to agree wholeheartedly.

Then just before I got into bed, I slipped a tape of *Dark Victory* into our VCR.

"What are you going to watch?" John asked, looking up from one of his research books on tornadoes.

I snuggled down into the covers and said, "*Dark Victory*."

"What!" John exploded. "That old turkey I saw years ago?"

"It's a classic," I said.

"A classic in morbidity!" John said. "I was depressed for two decades after. I'm still depressed because of that movie."

"Will you stop," I said. "It's not at all depressing. Actually it's quite heartening. Especially the last scene, where Judith—blind and dying—discovers that she has jammed a whole lifetime of happiness in a few borrowed months."

John barely let me finish the sentence. He cut in to say, "You're a sick woman, Liz."

When John got into one of his contentious moods, it didn't pay to argue. I just let him ramble on while I watched the screen credits roll.

"Look, Liz," John said, "I practically broke my kneecap running up the stairs to escape that she-wolf. Now you expect me to suffer through two hours of her flouncing across the screen, bullying all her coactors?"

All this was going through my mind as I signed my American Express slip at Pierre's. As Bette and I left the restaurant, I hoped that Grover had kept his promise to repair her bed.

We pulled into the driveway to discover Grover loading his truck. He stopped what he was doing and swept over to the car. With a princely gesture, he opened the door for Bette to get out.

"Miss Davis," Grover said, "your bed is fully repaired. It's no longer a ski slope." Then he added: "Skipper's just sweeping up the sawdust."

Bette passed that one off with an abrupt, "Hummmph." Then she said, "Liz, I want to give you a check for the lunch. Come with me."

I was going to refuse it, but I mentally compared her budget with mine and followed her into the bedroom.

I was shocked to see Skipper meticulously spreading Bette's wrinkled sheets out on the bed. He seemed to have the artistic passion of a great sculptor. Carefully, he folded hospital corners and then smoothed the sheets again and again, caressing away the smallest wrinkle with his shop-worn hands.

Bette stopped in her tracks as Skipper pointed out the hospital corners with pride. Then he looked at Bette wistfully and smoothed the pillow.

Bette turned to me with the eyes of a glacier and barked: "Elizabeth, I shall want fresh sheets immediately! And arrange for this inept bellboy to get the hell out of here!"

Skipper, drained of all his machismo, dropped one shoulder and curled it toward the door as he slunk out of the room.

Three times I apologized for Skipper's impertinence, and three times Bette gave me a frosty glare. She did, however, also give me the check for our lunch.

While Bette sat at her desk reading her manuscript over, I put clean sheets on her bed. She offered to help, but I told her that I really enjoyed making beds. Once again she gave me a frosty glare. Afterward I went into the kitchen, where Grover was having a toasted bagel.

"What in the hell happened in there?" Grover asked. Then he added, "Skipper just came out the door looking like he lost his best friend."

"Skipper was making Bette's bed and she threw him out."

"Did he short-sheet it?" Grover asked.

"No," I said, "but his enthusiasm for hospital corners triggered a primal scream."

"That guy's got it bad," Grover said, amused by Skipper's infatuation.

"Get serious, Grover. We've got a problem."

"*We've* got a problem?" Grover said. "It's clearly Skipper's problem."

I looked around the corner to make sure Bette wasn't coming. Then I whispered, "When I changed her pillow case, I found this note from Skipper inside it:

Dear Betty:
I hammer much better when I am in the same house as you and I will be true.
                    Luv,
                    Skipper"

Grover chuckled. "For a seventy-four-year-old, he's as horny as a Texas toad. But help is hard to find these days."

I slipped the note back in my pocket and told Grover, "You've got to tell him to knock it off."

"I say he should go for it!" Grover said with a smirk as he took a bite of his bagel.

"Don't joke," I said. "Right now Bette is in her room huffing and puffing."

"Tell her to take it easy," Grover said. "It wouldn't take much to blow this shack down."

"You don't think Bette would give Skipper a second look, do you?" I asked.

"I don't see anybody else beating down the door to get to her."

No sooner had Grover said those words when

the phone rang. United Press International was on the line. The UPI reporter asked to speak with Miss Bette Davis. This was an obvious security leak. How we had stayed anonymous for this length of time, I could never guess.

13

PHONE CALL
FROM A STRANGER

M y first mistake was to admit to the UPI reporter that Bette Davis was staying with us. My
second mistake was to admit to Bette that I was
aware that a reporter had called her. A reaction
wasn't long in coming.

"Elizabeth!" Bette bellowed the moment she hung
up the phone, "I need to talk to you at once!"

I braced myself. Then I slunk sheepishly into
her chamber—or what John called "the chamber
of horrors."

Bette was pacing. Her cigarette was dangerously
close to the draperies again. It crossed my mind
that I should always keep a bucket of water hidden
behind the draperies so that I could quickly put out
small fires from runaway cigarettes.

"That was United Press," Bette said.

"I know that." I hesitated.

Suddenly Bette stopped cold. She sucked in her cheeks, positioned the cigarette two inches from her freshly applied lipstick, and said in her usual clipped and exaggerated manner: "You-knew-that-a-reporter-was-on-the-phone-and-you-*STILL*-called-me-to-the-phone?"

"God," I said, "that was really stupid." I was so self-deprecating that she backed off.

"Well," Bette said, "what's done is done."

"I'll make sure that doesn't *ever* happen again," I reassured her.

"*Pleeeeze* do," she said. "We must avoid the media nosing around. They're *exhauuusting*! Goddam vultures!"

I was dying to know what the reporter wanted, but I didn't dare come out directly and ask. Instead I repeated what Bette just said: "Goddam-vultures-is-what-they-are!" I stopped myself from rolling my hips and flailing my arms.

"*Vulllltures!*" Bette said, tossing a half-smoked cigarette out the deck door. It landed on the freshly stained deck. I watched it singe the wood. Grover, I thought, could touch it up later.

"Being world famous has its drawbacks," I said to Bette.

"Being a goddam *nobody* has its drawbacks!" Bette retorted.

"Right," I said. "I just heard an old-time boxer on TV say, 'I rather be a *has-been* than a *never was.*'"

I couldn't get a reading to tell if Bette liked that little quip or not. She appeared to be deep in her own thoughts.

Finally she erupted like Vesuvius. "Kee-ryst!" Bette spouted, "that goddam reporter probably wanted to hear that 'Bette Davis is slapping her daughter with a fat lawsuit for having written such a horrendous pack of lies!' Humphh! Or maybe Walter Winchell wanted me to tell him that 'I'm sitting here in the boondocks, boozing, brawling, and playing Scrabble with Satan'? Maybe I should have told him, 'I have decided to follow B. D.'s quaint wish and have turned my life over to Jesus. I am now spending my days on bony knees admitting that I am nothing but a goddam Sinner!' "

Bette's monologue was suddenly interrupted by the phone ringing. The call was for her. This time I carefully screened the caller. The man simply said his name was Jimmy and that he was an old friend of hers. Bette, thinking that it was Jimmy Stewart, got on the line. Two seconds later she slammed the phone down.

I guess it wasn't Jimmy Stewart, I thought.

"Elizabeth!" Bette said. "That was some pathetic mongrel on your local paper who said that he'd met me. He had the nerve to think I'd grant him an interview!"

"The nerve of him!" I said, clucking like the sycophant I was.

Bette resumed her chronic pacing. "So word of my whereabouts has gotten out!" she said with an odd mixture of delight and distress.

I reassured Bette that I had told absolutely nobody. That wasn't exactly the whole truth. But I was confident that the few people I had told would keep it under wraps. My mind flashed to

Christopher. Could he have been the informer?
God knows he has a mouth. Just the other day
when I picked him up at preschool, he announced
loud and clear: "Mommy, we're going to go home
and see Bette Davis now."

One of the mothers overheard this and said, "Oh,
is she on TV today?"

"No," Christopher said. "She doesn't watch TV
during the day. Bette Davis is going to color with
me."

To throw her off the track, I said, "His new
babysitter is Betty Davis. Spelled with a *Y* not
an *E*."

The mother plucked her daughter's lunch box out
of a cubbyhole and said, "You know, the *real* Bette
Davis used to live here in Westport. On Crooked
Mile."

"I heard that," I said, also reaching for my child's
malodorous lunch box.

A very superior look came over the mother as she
told me, "My husband's aunt's best friend used to
live down the road from her. She said she was just
awful!"

Christopher, who had been taking in every word,
piped up, "Bette Davis is *not* awful. She's my bestess
friend!"

I comforted myself with the fact that even if
Christopher did say something, nobody would ever
believe a four-year-old. Then I thought: Maybe Skipper spilled the beans? When I brought this up to
Grover he became defensive.

"Skipper is closemouthed," he said. "We do lots
of work for the 'rich and famous.' "

It suddenly occurred to me that Grover might be the culprit in this security leak. But Grover was so sensitive over any sort of criticism, I decided discretion was the better part of valor. I pointed no finger, but merely suggested to Grover that perhaps he could remind Skipper that nobody was supposed to know where Bette Davis was staying. Grover agreed, then he went right on to tell me that the door frame in my office needed to be replaced.

I was only half listening to Grover. My mind had wandered to an unpleasant incident that had happened over the weekend. Our babysitter's girlfriend had told her parents that Bette Davis was staying in our house. The next day a car pulled into the driveway. A girl blasted out of her car and through our front door to where Bette was resting in her room. The girl, seeing Bette in bed, turned and ran back to her car screaming: "I saw her! I saw her!"

What followed was an even more disturbing incident for Bette. This time it involved door-to-door Jehovah's Witnesses. Bette and I had just gotten into my car when I suddenly noticed an olive drab station wagon slow and then stop in front of our driveway, blocking me from pulling out. The car had New York license plates. I automatically assumed the two people in the car were lost and looking for directions. I called from my car, "Are you lost?" The driver, a man in his early twenties, called back, "Not no more!"

The next thing I knew, the man and a middle-aged woman were walking up my driveway. Both were dressed in Bible Belt brown—or as Bette later said, "shit-brindle." Tucked under the man's arm was a floppy leather Bible. The woman carried a large handbag overflowing with pamphlets. The man worked my window and the woman went to Bette's window.

Immediately Bette began to roll up her window in the woman's face. But before Bette could get the window even halfway up, the woman slipped her hand inside the car, dropping a wad of pamphlets onto Bette's lap, saying, "Hasn't the Lord given us a beautiful day?"

"*Keee-ryst!*" Bette roared as she watched the pamphlets float to her lap. "What the hell's all this crap?"

I whispered to Bette, "They're Jehovah's Witnesses. My road is one of their regular rounds. If you're politely firm they'll go away."

On hearing that, Bette brushed the pamphlets off her lap onto the floor of the car and gave an exaggerated, "Phfffff!"

They didn't seem to know Bette. She was wearing dark glasses and a large-brimmed hat. But I doubt they would have recognized her even without the disguise.

"Listen," I said, "we're in a big hurry. We can't talk now."

My words carried no weight. Their heels were planted firmly in my gravel driveway. Their faces were poking through our windows. The Jehovah's Witness on Bette's side asked: "Are you a member of any church?"

For a split second I was afraid Bette was going to put her cigarette out in the woman's eye. But Bette jerked her head and cigarette toward me and ordered, "Step on it, sister!"

To keep Bette happy, I gunned the engine. I couldn't back up, however, because the man at my window had practically his entire arm stuck through my window, resting his worn Bible on my steering wheel. He was reciting some passage about floods, earthquakes, fires, all the usual stuff. I said to him: "We really must be on our way. Could you *please* move your car?"

The woman piped up and said, "Our Lord can move mountains."

To which Bette replied, "For chrissake, we're not asking the Lord to move mountains, we're asking you to move your goddam car!"

I thought Bette's tongue would have shocked them into moving on to a neighbor's house, but they didn't budge. The woman working Bette's window became more aggressive in her approach.

"Have you read His word?" the woman wanted to know.

Bette blasted: "Is this broad deaf?"

Still the woman was unshaken. "His word is the *only* word that can save your soul."

"Brother, she is deaf," Bette muttered.

The woman continued, "I speak to people all the time who never get nowhere . . ."

Now I was one hundred percent certain she didn't know to whom she was talking.

Bette was florid. She was rolling up her window at full speed, trying to beat out the woman, who was shoving more literature through a tiny opening at the top of the window. Pamphlets were sticking half in and half out as we pulled out of the driveway.

Recalling all of this prompted me to remind Grover once again that we must take all precautions to preserve Bette's privacy. Once again, Grover gave me his Yankee word that he would have a talk with Skipper before the day was over.

Less than twenty-four hours later, Skipper was banging on my office door.

"Pardon me," he said, out of breath. "I need to talk to you, Mrs. Fuller!"

"Come on in," I said, expecting to hear almost anything.

"I was out front diggin' a hole for your post fence, when all of a sudden a big white Caddy pulls up and a lady sittin' behind the wheel says to me, 'Can you tell me which house Bette Davis is stayin' in?' "

"Oh no!" I wailed.

Skipper continued, still out of breath. "I see a camera on the dashboard and I says to her and her lady friend, 'State your business.' The lady says she just wants to get a picture of the house Bette Davis is stayin' in.' And I says to her, 'There ain't nobody by that name stayin' in this here house.' "

I interrupted Skipper to say, "That was just the perfect reply."

Skipper, puffed up with my praise, went on, "Then she shows me a newspaper clippin' with your street address, and sure enough it says that Bette Davis is stayin' right here!"

Then Skipper poked his head out the door and said, "There goes that Caddy now. It's goin' slow as a snail."

The rest of the afternoon Skipper kept track of any car or pedestrian who looked the least bit suspicious.

At the end of the day he reported back to me.

Skipper's timing could not have been worse. Bette had just settled down at her favorite nook with her nightly wine spritzer. Christopher was engrossed with TV, watching Mr. Rogers and, as Bette said, "His visit to a goddam marble factory." Grover had turned my kitchen bar into his office. John was across from him, bickering over a bill. I was hunched over the stove preparing three different dinners: hot dogs for Christopher, leftover chili for John, and Stouffers frozen dinners for Bette and me.

As if all this confusion wasn't enough, Skipper whipped a folded sheet of paper out of his shirt pocket. The paper listed all the suspicious traffic going past our house.

"At approximately 2:38 P.M.," Skipper read, loud enough for his Golden Girl to hear, "a black Honda Accord slowed to approximately ten miles per hour as it neared the house . . ."

Grover cut in, "Why do I feel like this is Mayberry USA?"

" . . . the vehicle bearing Connecticut plates DYP-450, carried a single white male, approximately forty years of age . . ."

Listening to this mock police report, John tossed aside Grover's bill and called to me, "What the hell is he talking about?"

I hadn't yet told John about the "security leak," nor had I told Bette that Skipper had designated himself her gentleman-at-arms. Now was not the time to tell either of them anything.

I whispered to John, "I'll explain everything later."

It was difficult to tell if Bette could actually hear Skipper over the TV noise of Mr. Rogers. It was also hard to tell whom Bette suddenly had more disdain for: Mr. Rogers and his "goddam sneakers" or Skipper, whom she refused to look at.

Skipper continued reading his report: "Between 4:06 and 4:49 a white female approximately thirty years of age, on foot, pushing a baby coach eastbound."

I stopped him. "That's Margaret, who lives down the street with her new baby."

Reluctantly Skipper crossed off her name from his "most wanted" list and then went on: "At approximately 5:10, a white female on foot, connected to a large white dog, lingered suspicious-like by your oak tree—"

Once again I stopped Skipper. "That was Bonnie and her dog, Shep. He likes my tree."

"Skipper," Grover said, laughing, "I'm going to book you on a G-2."

"What's a G-2?" I asked, looking over at Bette. There was a frightening stillness about her.

Grover took a swig of his Budweiser and said, "Military Intelligence."

"That's an oxymoron if I ever heard one," John said, drawing a poisonous grin from Bette.

Skipper continued: "At approximately 5:35 P.M., a slender—"

To keep a lid on Bette, I interrupted Skipper: "Well supper's ready," I said, calling Bette, Christopher, and John to the table.

Skipper appeared disappointed that I had cut him off so rudely. He shrugged his shoulders as if to say, "Ingrate." Then he folded his "report" and tucked it back into his pocket. On his way out the door he gave Bette a wink and said, "I'll be keepin' close surveillance on this here place, Miss Davis."

Bette recoiled and said to Grover: "It's time for the men in the white ice cream suits to haul this asshole away!"

Fortunately for Skipper he was already out the door when Bette vented. Christopher, however, was in hearing range.

"Mommy," Christopher said, "tell Bette Davis not to use the 'A' word!"

Supper was uneventful. Bette didn't bring up the security leak. John didn't moan over the fact that Grover had just discovered that we needed all new sills and girders. And I didn't bring up the fact that two other newspapers had called in the last hour to speak to Bette Davis.

The only tense moment came when Christopher refused to eat his hot dog because it was in a hamburger bun.

"Liz," John said, "if he doesn't eat his hot dog then he doesn't get a popsicle for dessert!"

When that had absolutely no effect on Chris, I raised my voice and threatened: "No hot dog, no TV tonight!"

"I hate popsicles and I hate TV!" he said, folding his arms and throwing out his lower lip.

Bette moved in like a pro. "I suppose you hate Superman, too," she said, going for his weak spot.

"I love Superman," Christopher said, falling into her trap.

"When I made my last film at the Disney Studio, I had *lunch* with Superman," Bette said, looking at Christopher out of the corner of her eye.

Christopher's lower lip retracted.

"Superman ordered his hot dog on a hamburger roll," Bette said.

Christopher's moist eyes began to glisten. "But you're not supposed to eat hot dogs on hamburger buns," he spouted.

Bette nodded her head in agreement. "That's right, Master Fuller. Not unless you're Superman."

A mischievous glint came over Christopher's face. "Well I can eat it that way *too*," he said, devouring the hot dog in the hamburger roll.

As soon as we finished eating, Christopher ran to his bedroom to put on his Superman pajamas. Bette went into her room to get her manuscript. John threw another log on the fire to take the chill off the cool June evening, and I made coffee.

"I thought maybe you'd enjoy hearing what I wrote today, Elizabeth," Bette said, slipping on her glasses.

With a crackling fire, Bette began to read from her yellow tablet. "Crawford was consistent in her vanity," she read, deciphering her handwriting. "Miss Crawford owned *threeeee* sizes of bosoms—"

I cut Bette off: "Is that true?"

Bette dropped the yellow pad to her lap and blasted, "I just said it was *true*! Didn't I?"

As Bette prepared to read on, Christopher bolted into the living room. He began to leap on and off the sofa opposite Bette, his red Superman cape dangling behind him. Immediately I swept him up and put him to bed. By the time I came back downstairs, Bette had lost interest in reading to us. In fact she lost interest in even talking to us.

"I'm exhausted," she said. Her eyes, however, defied her words. I figured she would be up half the night smoking and watching Carson and then old movies. John and I could hear the TV set beside her bed going to the wee hours of the morning practically every night.

"Good night," Bette said, snatching up her cigarette case, yellow pad, and a handful of cookies.

"Sleep tight. Don't let the bed bugs bite," I said, suddenly admonishing myself for sounding like a flaming "A" word.

Bette either didn't hear me or she was graciously allowing it to pass without comment. "Darlings," she said at the door leading to her room, "I *desperately* need to send this manuscript to New York, and I don't want it to go by Pony Express for godsakes!"

John poked the fire and said, "Federal Express. It's guaranteed overnight delivery."

"Terrific!" she said.

"I'll give you the 800 number at breakfast," I said.

"Please do. I *need* to have it at the publishers by Friday."

"Tomorrow's already Thursday," I said. Bette gave me her famous deadpan expression. Her look gave me a bit of a shiver when I thought what might happen if her manuscript failed to arrive on time.

"Oh and one other thing, Liz," Bette said. "I need to borrow an iron."

I thought: An iron? Bette Davis is going to *iron* her clothes? This was not an easy image to conjure up.

"You need an iron?" I asked, thinking that I must have misunderstood her.

"That's what I just said," Bette grumbled.

"Miss Davis," I said, feeling the muscles around my jaw tighten, "you're going to think this is a bit strange, but I don't have an iron."

I explained how as a teenager one of my chores was to do the family ironing. I vowed that when I grew up I'd have a maid or wear wrinkled clothes, which I preferred anyway. It was more *me*.

Bette's response was to arch her Estée Lauder eyebrows.

I quickly added, "I can borrow an iron from my neighbor across the road."

"Thank you, darling," Bette said, so forgiving that my tension headache actually lifted.

I looked out the window toward our neighbor's house, a tidy gray clapboard with window boxes overflowing with geraniums. Since their lights were still on I decided to call and ask if I could trouble them for an iron and ironing board. I didn't mention whom it was for. They were an elderly Yankee couple who, although neighborly, kept to themselves. I doubted if they even knew Bette Davis was staying with us.

Within minutes Harold Keene was at my front door. He insisted on bringing the iron over and showing me exactly how it worked.

When Harold came in, Bette was standing at the kitchen sink taking her pills. I introduced them to each other. Harold didn't bat an eyelash. I thought that he might have missed the name, because he was practically deaf. Or maybe he just wasn't interested in Living Legends?

Harold set up the old metal ironing board. He warned us three times not to get our fingers pinched in the rusty metal clasp. Then he showed Bette how to use the steam iron his wife, Ethel, had just ordered from the Sears catalogue.

"Where's the linen dial?" Bette asked as she slipped on her heavy-frame glasses.

"The what dial?" Harold screamed in his hard-of-hearing decibels.

"The linen dial," Bette screamed back amiably.

"I can't hardly see this dang thing without my glasses," Harold yelled.

"Here, use these," Bette said, passing her glasses to a fellow Yankee.

Harold slipped them on and showed Bette the linen dial. "You gotta fill this contraption with water," he warned.

"How much water?" Bette wanted to know.

"About a measurin' cup," Harold told her.

As I watched the star of the silver screen totally absorbed with a Sears iron, I thought about how my grandmother and I had fantasized Bette Davis's life. We didn't even come close to the scene that was now playing before my eyes—Bette Davis ironing her clothes in my own living room?

While I was deep in this thought, Harold turned to me and hollered: "What happened to your iron, Missy?"

Harold always called me Missy. To avoid a long explanation, I simply hollered back: "It's broken."

"It's broke?" Harold asked as Bette predictably rolled her eyes. Then he said, "Give it to me, Missy. I'll take it home and see if it can be fixed."

Harold had a knack for being able to fix anything. In fact, fifty years earlier he and Ethel had actually built their own house across the road, board by board, plumbing and all.

I was just about to tell Harold that I had thrown it away when Bette piped in. "We threw the iron in the trash last week," she said, winking at me.

Not only was our friendship on a definite roll, but we were beginning to read each other.

I winked back at Bette and repeated: "Yeah, the trash man hauled it away last week."

At four-thirty the following afternoon, I arrived home from the grocery store. Bette was standing in front of the ironing board, pressing a French cuff on one of her tailored white shirts.

"Federal Express promised they'd pick up this manuscript before *five*," she said, slamming down the iron.

"I'll call them right now," I said.

As I picked up the phone I had a sudden sick feeling in the pit of my stomach. Maybe I had grounds for that sick feeling?

Federal Express informed me that they *had* arrived at our house at two-thirty, but they were turned away by the "caretaker." I asked if they could come back, and they told me that they made *no* home pickups after five o'clock. It was almost five now.

I hung up the phone and immediately summoned Skipper into the house. When Skipper began to recap the story of how he had dismissed the Federal Express truck, Bette burst into the wild-eyed look of a cavewoman out on a kill.

Skipper turned to read from his notepad: "At 0230 hours, a truck bearin' the name Federal Express pulls into driveway. I put down my shovel and go over to the driver and I says: 'Afternoon, sir. What can I do for you?' The driver says: 'I'm here to pick up a package from a Miss B. Davis' . . ."

I didn't have the courage to look at Bette. I could hear her puffing savagely on her cigarette. I prayed for one of her lethal cracks to break the tension.

Skipper, convinced that he had saved the day, went on: "There was somethin' not right about the driver. His uniform was lookin' too big and it had a military press. I once had a friend who worked for United Parcel and he never had no military press on his uniform. I start thinkin' that maybe the real driver is tied up in the bushes somewheres. I seen that in the movies . . ."

Bette stood by in deep shock. There was an ominous chill in the room as Skipper went on to say, "I says to this bogus Federal Express driver: 'There ain't nobody by that name in this house' . . ."

I could remain silent no longer. "Skipper," I roared, "Miss Davis has been waiting all day for that Federal Express truck!"

Skipper looked as if someone had punctured him with a knitting needle. "Nobody told me nothin' about that," he said, down and dejected.

At last Bette spoke: "Elizabeth, this clown should have someone do his arguing for him!" Then she gave him one final killer glare and stormed out of the room, slamming the door behind her.

Bette didn't come out of her room for cocktail hour or even for dinner. She said that she was too upset to eat. I knew better than to press the issue. I also knew she wasn't going to starve to death. She had several boxes of cookies stashed in the desk drawer.

Then at quarter to nine that same evening Bette burst into the living room. She was waving the *TV Guide*.

"Elizabeth!" she said. "*Jezebel*'s going to be on the late TV movie tonight. I know it's your favorite movie. I thought we could watch it together."

"I'll make popcorn," I said, soaring.

"First I need to get some dinner," Bette said as she walked into the kitchen and searched the freezer for a Stouffers macaroni and cheese.

With Bette out of hearing range, John whispered, "I'm not going to sit through an endless parade of maudlin slush."

I whispered back, "She didn't ask you to watch it. She only asked *me!*"

"Liz," John said in a hushed voice, "this hero worship doesn't become you. She's camped here now for twenty-six days and two eons, and you're getting worse by the hour."

14

JEZEBEL

Everything in the room appeared surrealistic as I sat down next to Bette to watch *Jezebel*, "the film." Resting on the coffee table was a bowl of buttered popcorn fighting for attention over the cigarette smoke. As the music and credits faded in and out, Bette tucked her feet underneath her robe.

"Willie Wyler was a *genius!*" she said about the director whom she had taken up with during the filming of *Jezebel*. These were the last days of her marriage to husband number one.

"*He's* the man I should have married," Bette said, as if she had just made that massive discovery while looking at his screen credit on our twenty-one-inch Sony.

Then without missing a beat, Bette went on, "Haller was a brilliant photographer! He knew lighting. Gawd, today they don't know shit from Shinola."

As Ernie Haller's name rolled off the screen, I was trying to figure a way to steer the monologue onto Henry Fonda—her male lead as Pres Dillard. For years my grandmother and I had agonized over whether Bette had actually been in love with Fonda the way Miss Julie had been in love with Pres.

While Bette reminisced about the tedious costume fittings, I privately reminisced about how my grandmother's hairdresser friend, Mildred, had long ago told us that Bette Davis had had an affair with Fonda during the making of *Jezebel* and that's what broke up Bette's first marriage and soured the next three. Of course my grandmother and I took whatever Mildred told us about movie stars with a grain of salt. We relied a hundred percent on the movie magazines for the TRUTH.

Now, sitting in the darkened room beside Jezebel herself, it took all my self-control to refrain from asking personal questions.

After a long bout of silence, Bette spoke. *"Therrre's* a defiant, daring little bitch," she said approvingly as she watched her character flounce off her horse and into her antebellum mansion. Dressed in a riding habit, Miss Julie shocked all the southern ladies, who were in proper dress for an afternoon tea in 1850.

"I just love how Miss Julie lifts her cape with one snotty flick of her riding crop," I said to Bette, who took a deep, appreciative drag on her cigarette, scrutinizing that scene through widened eyes.

"That gesture, darling, was the single most effective use of body language to establish my character." Then she added forcefully, "That was *Wyler's* brilliance! It still burns me that he didn't get best director."

"But you got best actress," I piped in, more for myself than for her. *I* was sitting beside Jezebel. Me, the daring and defiant little bitch from Cleveland who was Bette Davis's soul mate, only she didn't realize this on a conscious level yet. Perhaps, I thought, now was the time to clue her in.

"You know, Miss Davis," I spoke with hesitation, "in so many ways I think we're actually a lot alike."

I couldn't tell if she registered those words. Her eyes were bugged half out of their sockets as she watched Pres give Miss Julie a tongue-lashing. It suddenly occurred to me that maybe Mildred had been right about Hank and Bette after all.

I considered repeating myself but then I decided not to push it. At the moment, Bette appeared some-what aloof. I told myself that a healthy friendship has a balance of closeness and distance. I would keep my questions impersonal.

"How'd you ever cultivate such an authentic southern accent?" I asked. But instead of getting an answer, I got a demonstration.

Bette immediately repeated the lines on the screen as they were spoken. "Pres, let me go. Take me out of here," Bette said, with all the inflection of the publicly humiliated Miss Julie.

"That accent's amazing!" I said.

"Wyler brought in a voice coach from a southern university for Hank and me," Bette said, taking a sip of her wine spritzer.

"We should be drinking mint juleps," I said in an embarrassingly bad southern accent. Bette ignored me. Her entire being was focused on the memorable ballroom scene where Miss Julie creates a sensation in her scarlet dress.

"What a scene!" I said, scooping up the last of the popcorn.

"Fonda and I did that ballroom scene for a solid week. Originally it was supposed to have been shot in a half day. But Wyler wasn't going to throw it away."

"Well, it certainly paid off," I said, practically drooling.

"Of course it paid off for godsakes!"

Then I said something that nearly cost me my life.

"I'm sure Miss Julie was deeply in love with Pres."

"*That's* what the whole goddam movie is all about!" Bette said, spitting fire.

"Well I know that," I said somewhat defensively. "I guess what I meant to say was that Miss Julie was such a strong-willed character that I'm sure she would go on to live happily ever after with or without Pres."

"What do you mean, live happily ever after? The goddam movie ends with her being madly in love with Pres and Pres being in love with his new wife!"

"Yes, I know that," I said, backed into a corner. "But whenever I used to see *Jezebel*, I would always fantasize what happened afterward. I would make up many more new scenes."

"Well there ain't no *Jezebel II*, sister!"

"Yes!" I said. "Anything else would be a pale imitation." I added, "The heartrending unrequited love Miss Julie had for Pres—it just wouldn't have been as effective if Julie had gotten Pres."

"Unrequited love is *murrrder!*" Bette said as if she were drawing on real-life experience. "Pres was going to kick the bucket, and Miss Julie would be rambling around in her family estate alone and miserable."

"Miss Davis," I blurted out, "I think you're doing the same thing I'm guilty of: fantasizing what happens to the characters after the movie ends."

"Fantasize nothing!" Bette cut in. "I was thinking of that miserable cold I caught after the movie ended—thanks to Wyler and his penchant for realism. He had me working twenty-hour days to complete that film. That river scene was shot at midnight! I was covered in water and mud in order to look as if I had trudged miles to get to that lug Pres, who was supposed to have been infected with Yellow Jack. I almost died after the filming. I was physically and mentally exhausted. *Gawd*, I just love those people who are always telling me what I'm thinking!"

"I didn't mean to sound as if I were telling you—"

Bette interrupted. "I was at a party one evening," she said, with her eyes still on the TV screen, "and Hedda Hopper came up to me and said in her bitchy, confidential tone: 'Bette, darling, I just saw *Jezebel*. You were magnificent! But there's no hiding that you're in love with Hank. It was written all over your face.' "

I interjected, "The nerve of Hedda Hopper!"

"Brother," Bette said, "she could be a bitch."

"I think that perhaps Hedda Hopper got that

impression," I told Bette thoughtfully, "because you played Miss Julie with such power. Such realism. The sign of a truly great actor!" Then I held my breath and waited to be either blasted off earth for my impertinence, or for Bette to suddenly spill out her guts about her affair with Hank Fonda. As I waited for her response, I wished that every person who had ever snubbed me could see me now—sitting inches away from Jezebel, critiquing her movie like Siskel and Ebert, and bad-rapping the late, great Hedda Hopper with the Flick Queen.

After what seemed like an eternity, Bette spoke: "Hopper got that impression because I *was* in love. I was in love with *Wyler!* Hopper didn't know that all those close-ups of me looking at Fonda had been taken after he left the lot to be with his wife in New York. His wife was pregnant with Jane. During those close-ups I was looking at *Wyler* off-camera. Hank had the looks, but Wyler had all the rest!"

"I've always been attracted to rather seedy looking men, too," I said.

"Seedy!" Bette sneered. "Who said Wyler was seedy?"

"I guess I meant to say that he was no Gable."

"Thank God he was no Gable!" Bette said as she smashed out her cigarette, upsetting the ashtray.

"I've never been taken with Gable either," I muttered, sweeping up the ashes and cigarette butts from the rug with my Dustbuster.

During the commercial I broke the deadly silence by telling Bette, "Probably the most revealing line about Miss Julie's character is when her devoted Aunt Belle says of her: 'I love her most when she's her meanest, because I know that's when she's lovin' most.' "

Bette gave a double take, surprised that I had that line memorized.

"So you've seen this movie a few times before?" Bette asked in an unexpectedly benevolent tone.

"At least a dozen times," I told her. "Most of those times with my grandmother."

"Before she died, I hope," Bette quipped.

I couldn't help but wonder if *anything* I had told her about the spirit world had sunk in. I guessed not. She was a hard-core realist—except when it came to love, as she was soon to divulge.

I watched Bette's eyes as she watched the TV screen. They were intent on Miss Julie, humbling herself before Pres: "Pres, I'm kneelin' to yah," Miss Julie said in a last-ditch attempt to win back Pres.

"That's a powerful scene," I said to Bette, who nodded agreeably.

Then Bette spewed forth: "If I could live my life all over again, I'd *nevvvver* let a man have all of me. They're goddam vultures! The second they know they have you hooked, the game's over and they're onto their next conquest."

"But you've always had your work," I said.

Once again Bette nodded congenially.

"My grandmother really hated men too," I said.

"Who said I hated men?" Bette snarled. "I loved them *too* much, for chrissake!"

"That's dangerous," I said.

"It's *disastrous!*" Bette agreed.

"I think Miss Julie loved Pres too much," I said.

"She loved what she couldn't possess," Bette said

in a flat tone. "In that regard we were the same."

"Maybe that's the human condition," I said, adding, "loving that which you can't have."

"Perhaps," Bette said. "God, how I loved strong men. But I married a string of nonentities. They became *Mr*. Bette Davis! Except for Merrill. *He* was different."

"I always thought of Spencer Tracy as one of Hollywood's strong men," I said, wondering why Bette had never considered him for marriage.

"A *drunk*!" Bette snapped.

"Katharine Hepburn certainly must have found something attractive about him," I said, a little shocked that I dared to speak up.

"He was attractive, all right," Bette retorted. "And he knew it. Tracy had everybody."

"Did Hepburn know that?" I asked.

Bette took a lung-searing drag on her cigarette and said, "She was no virgin."

"Sounds as if Hollywood was a pretty exciting place to be back in the thirties and forties," I said, thinking how dull Cleveland Heights was in the early sixties when I was doing the Mashed Potato to Dee-Dee Sharp at Teen Town, where chaperones were positioned like guards at Riker's Island.

"Everybody was shacked up with everybody else," Bette said, suddenly sounding like an Alabama Bible school teacher.

"Were *any* of the greats faithful?" I wanted to know.

"Bette's answer was quick: "*I* was faithful. Whenever I was in love, I gave it my all. I overwhelmed them!"

"Same here," I said as I cracked open the sliding glass door to get rid of some of the cigarette smoke that was literally making me dizzy. "Before I got married, all my lovers complained that I overwhelmed them." I really had only two: a junior high school gym teacher and a flight engineer with sweaty hands.

Bette made no comment. I didn't expect her to. But I felt by the way she studied my face that she was beginning to see that there were definite similarities in our personalities: we were both strong women who dared to love too much.

During the final scenes on the TV screen, I couldn't take my eyes off Bette. I was hardly paying attention to Miss Julie. I was fascinated with the real Miss Julie sitting less than two feet away from me, chain-smoking and crunching small pieces of ice between her teeth as she watched Miss Julie drag herself halfway across New Orleans to get to the dying Pres.

"This is the best part of the entire movie," I said sweetly.

Bette nodded.

After the screen faded to black, I asked, "Do you want to switch to the last part of Johnny Carson?"

"Not me, darling," Bette said, plucking up her cigarettes and Bic lighter. "That movie *exhausted* me. I'm going straight to bed."

Later that evening I could hear her through our thin antique walls as she chuckled with muffled laughter over the antics of the David Letterman show. I fell asleep that night thinking about my grandmother and how we used to light candles in church for everything and anything. Half the time my grandmother would light the candles without even dropping in a dime through the metal slot, saying that she was saving every penny for our trip to California. Mostly my grandmother and I planned this vacation while on the bus going to our local movie theater. My grandmother would fill me with stories on how we could actually participate in a souvenir film at the studios. Mildred's sister did that and it cost her ten dollars. The first day we were there we would have lunch at Schwabs Drug Store where I might even get discovered because I was certainly as beautiful as all the others. And of course we would go to the Farmer's Market where all the movies stars shopped. But the highlight of our trip would be to take the bus tour to see where Bette Davis lived.

When our family finally did take that trip, my grandmother had been too frail to go along. But I brought her back postcards, souvenirs and photographs. Her favorite was a photograph of me in front of Graumann's Chinese Theater. I was standing behind the Bette Davis footprint, dramatically posing with my mother's cigarette as a prop.

Over the next few years my grandmother's condition worsened but her mind remained alert. Only weeks before she died I had taken her to the drive-in movie to see *It's a Mad, Mad, Mad, Mad World* that starred Spencer Tracy, my grandmother's favorite male actor whom she always felt belonged more with Bette Davis than Katharine Hepburn.

After my grandmother's funeral we went back to my Aunt Ruth's house where my grandmother had lived. I went into her bedroom and Scotch taped to her dresser mirror was that photograph of me taken in front of Graumann's Chinese Theater. The Scotch tape was all brown and curled at the edges. Resting in a little cedar box that said "Welcome to Universal Studio" were my airline wings. I had told my supervisor that I had lost mine so that I could send them to my grandmother. She was so proud of me and told everybody that her granddaughter was a stewardess and flew to California whenever she felt like it.

Now as I drifted off to sleep I could still hear the sounds of Bette's TV, and I thought that if I could have one wish it would be for my grandmother to be here with me to hear Bette Davis chuckling in my very own house.

15

ME AND JEZEBEL

It was four days after that memorable evening of watching *Jezebel* that Bette came into the kitchen and announced that she would be leaving the following morning.

"The hotel strike's over!" Bette called as she burst through her bedroom door. "The limo shall be here at ten o'clock tomorrow morning."

Those words hit with more intensity than any of her other words over the past month. This was the final curtain for me and Jezebel. And I was never much good at final curtains.

"Well," I said, mustering up good cheer just as Miss Julie had done when she learned Pres had gotten married, "I'm making your favorite Boston baked bean dish for your last night here."

"*Splendid!*" Bette said, snapping her gold compact closed. "We'll celebrate. You're finally *rid* of me."

I wanted to say so much. I wanted to tell her that since her visit my life would never be the same again, that through her I was able to realize and accept the real me. Still fresh in my mind was what she had told me two evenings earlier, when I was in a silly mood and I did my Margo Channing imitation for her.

"Elizabeth," Bette said, moments after I finished, "you're *you* and I'm *me*. There's only *one* me. And there's only *one* you. Stop trying to be *me*! You're a damn good you!"

But instead of telling Bette how much those words meant to me I said: "I've remembered to use Colman's dry mustard."

"For godsakes don't overdo it," she scolded. "And what about the molasses?"

"It's right here," I said. Then I reached into the cupboard, only to come face to face with her Carnation Instant Breakfast drink. Suddenly I felt my heart race and then skip a beat, recalling all those mornings when I'd come into the kitchen to find Bette sipping her breakfast drink, reading the *Daily News* and suffering Grover and Skipper.

As I mixed two cans of B&M baked beans, a teaspoon of Colman's, and half a cup of molasses into a crock, it occurred to me that maybe everything that needed to be said had already been said.

On the morning of Bette's departure, several cubic meters of luggage were neatly packed and ready for their transportation to New York. This consisted of one stretch limo for Bette and driver and one station wagon with chauffeur exclusively for her luggage.

Grover arrived a half hour before Bette was due to leave. Although he had finally completed the renovations on our house, he came over to say good-bye to Bette. Fortunately he had the good sense not to tell Skipper that Bette was leaving.

Bette seemed pleased to see Grover. She especially seemed pleased Skipper wasn't with him.

"Grover," Bette said as he stepped through our front door, "if I ever buy another old house I will *insist* that you do the renovations."

Grover responded in his Yankee twang: "Well, Bette, there's no job too big or too small—too near or too far for us."

Bette snapped, "Just keep that Neanderthal sidekick of yours away from me!"

Grover chuckled. Even Bette managed a chuckle.

I watched the way Grover and Bette related to each other, and I thought about Bette and me never having had that free and easy rapport. Perhaps it was because I was never able to stop calling her Miss Davis. But it was more than that. Something deep inside of me prevented me from calling her Bette. I know now what it was. In a strange way I was preserving the memory of my grandmother. I was keeping alive that which we both held sacred: our devotion to the movies—and more specifically, to Bette Davis.

While Bette and Grover chatted about how the barn was America's greatest contribution to architecture the phone rang. It was Grace. She was calling to say good-bye to Bette.

Bette was reserved but congenial. "Grace," she

said, taking the phone from me, "I want to thank you for your thoughtfulness in bringing over that videotape of my daughter on that religious broadcast. That was *most* kind of you."

After Bette hung up the phone she turned to me and said, "Your Grace is quite a sincere woman."

"Oh," I said, "there's not a phony bone in her *entire* body." Then I asked, "Maybe when my book about her comes out you'll read it?"

Bette was noncommittal.

"And where is Sir John and Master Christopher?" Bette asked, looking at her watch. It was quarter to ten. The limo was due in fifteen minutes.

"They're outside," I said.

John had taken Christopher outside to keep him from jumping on and off Bette's luggage, which stood in the hallway.

"I must see my little boyfriend before I go," she said. Then she added, "I've autographed his play table."

"Christopher will be thrilled," I said, inspecting a white square of paper resting on top of the plastic table she used as her cocktail table. It read: "Thank you Chris for letting me share your table. Bette Davis."

Bette smoothed out her black tailored suit skirt and instructed: "You'll need scotch tape to hold it in place. You may see to that after I leave."

"That'll be a priority," I said to Bette, who was now counting her bags, making sure she had not forgotten anything.

Five minutes before the limo arrived, I called Christopher and John inside. Unlike John, Christopher was not at all pleased about "his" Bette Davis leaving.

"When you coming back, Bette Davis?" Christopher asked in a high-pitched whine, staring up at her with moist eyes.

Bette answered his question with a question: "Young man, how would you like 'Bette Davis' to leave my telephone number with your mother and father? You may phone me from time to time. We'll have a nice chat—all about Superman and Yabba-dabba-doo?"

A tentative smile came over Christopher's face. "Will you send me a big picture of you?"

Hearing my son ask Bette Davis for her picture was a bit startling. I had to smile, thinking that we may have a miniature Bette Davis fan in the works.

Bette told Christopher: "Master Fuller, I shall send you a big color picture of 'Bette Davis.' And inside will be your very own record album. You may play it on your Big Bird phonograph."

"Wow!" Christopher squealed, revealing a mouth full of baby teeth.

Even John grinned. At that very moment, nobody could have convinced me that John wasn't going to miss Bette just a little. I could read it in his eyes. Of course John would never admit to this. But little things he had said indicated otherwise.

As John was getting dressed for breakfast, he said to me, "I'm finally going to be able to finish my book in peace and quiet."

"Me too," I said, feeling a vacancy.

"Who knows," John said, "maybe there'll be

another hotel strike and we'll be saddled with her again."

"No chance," I said.

"Well, there's no way I could take another month with her barbed-wire personality," John said. Somehow he didn't sound as if he meant that.

"She's a woman who's not afraid to speak her mind. She's got the guts to say what the rest of us think," I said, choosing what I was going to wear for her send-off. I decided on a black T-shirt and baggy jeans. Bette once commented that I looked good in black.

"After today I'll be able to give up the Maalox," John said. He popped one in his mouth to get him through breakfast. A few moments later he added, "I've never before seen anyone with such an enriched capacity for enjoying conflict." He said that almost admiringly.

At ten o'clock sharp the stretch limo, followed by a nondescript station wagon, pulled into our driveway

"Bette Davis, your lemoneeze is here!" Christopher shouted from the window, where he was playing a game with Bette that they called "Who-can-spot-the-limousine-first?"

"So it is," Bette said, slipping on her white gloves, looking the part.

Christopher scrambled out the front door. John took off after him in hot pursuit. Bette, however, remained in the house with me as the two chauffeurs gathered the luggage in our hallway.

"Now darling," Bette said, pointing with her cigarette toward the kitchen phone, "I've scribbled a little note to you with my telephone number at the Ritz Carlton."

Resting on the kitchen counter was a sheet of Bette's yellow-lined paper. At the top was her telephone number, followed by a note. It read:

Never again say "yes"
to any request to
stay with you
During a strike,
As you now know
It is possible for
this guest
To stay for life!
              Much love always
              Chris's *Bette* Davis
              Give him a hug
              and a kiss for me.

With the note in my hand I stared at the last three lines. There was a softness and affection that belied the reputation that Bette desperately had lived up to.

Once again I was tempted to tell Bette how much her visit had meant to me. But I stopped myself from getting sloppy and said, "This dump is always open to you, Miss Davis."

"Thank you, darling," Bette chuckled as she walked toward the front door.

"I really mean that," I said, reaching out my hands toward hers. She took them with remarkable strength and gave me a hug and a squeeze good-bye.

Then I walked her slowly along the gravel drive-way. The chauffeur was holding the door of what seemed to be a land yacht open for her. John and Christopher were standing on the edge of the driveway as if they were farewell wishers for the *Q.E. II.*

As she stepped into the silver-gray limo, she blew them a kiss. Moments later both vehicles slowly backed out of the driveway and onto our narrow country road, to mark the end of a visit that, to say the least, was memorable.

I watched as the limo disappeared around a curve, and then I turned back toward the front door. I shook my head and said, almost aloud, *"Keee-ryst,* I'm going to miss that woman!"